MW00607666

796.83 B751o   38981

Brenner, Teddy.

Only the ring was square.

DISCARDED

LAWTON PUBLIC LIBRARY

ONLY THE RING WAS SQUARE

Teddy Brenner
as told to Barney Nagler

Prentice-Hall, Inc. Englewood Cliffs, New Jersey 07632

796.83
B7510

Book Designer: Donna Kurdock
Art Director: Hal Siegel

Only the Ring Was Square, by Teddy Brenner as told to Barney Nagler
Copyright © 1981 by Teddy Brenner and Barney Nagler

All rights reserved. No part of this book may be
reproduced in any form or by any means, except
for the inclusion of brief quotations in a review,
without permission in writing from the publisher.
Address inquiries to Prentice-Hall, Inc.,
Englewood Cliffs, New Jersey 07632
Printed in the United States of America
Prentice-Hall International, Inc., London
Prentice-Hall of Australia, Pty. Ltd., Sydney
Prentice-Hall of Canada, Ltd., Toronto
Prentice-Hall of India Private Ltd., New Delhi
Prentice-Hall of Japan, Inc., Tokyo
Prentice-Hall of Southeast Asia Pte. Ltd., Singapore
Whitehall Books Limited, Wellington, New Zealand

10 9 8 7 6 5 4 3 2 1

Library of Congress Cataloging in Publication Data

Brenner, Teddy.
  Only the ring was square.

  Includes index.
    1. Boxing—United States—History. 2. Brenner,
Teddy. 3. Matchmakers (Boxing)—United States—
Biography. I. Nagler, Barney. II. Title.
GV1125.B73   796.8'3'0973   81-5940
ISBN 0-13-637223-6   AACR2

Contents

For Punch and Judy and Pam and Barry

A Matter
of Principle

To the boys in boxing Eddie Walker was a philosopher. If he were alive today and heard people call him a philosopher he would turn over in his grave. He never intended to be a philosopher. He loved money too much.

How come he got a reputation for thinking was that he once said something smart. At least it sounded smart. Once you say something smart in boxing people get the idea that you think. Nothing you do after that will keep them from thinking you spend all your time thinking.

What Walker said, when he was managing fighters in the 40s, was that the first year you are in boxing you are in it for the money. After that you are in it for revenge. I do not hold with Eddie Walker's philosophy. I have been in boxing for forty years. For twenty of those years I was the matchmaker for Madison Square Garden. A matchmaker is a guy who starts fights and then gets out of the way.

The reason I do not agree with Walker's way of looking

at life, now that he is dead, is that it is not revenge that keeps a guy in boxing. It is money, like if you are in oil or banking or bookmaking. Money and pride. Pride is the big thing.

Take Eddie Borden. Until they had a falling out, Borden was one of Eddie Walker's closest pals. Borden was a boxing hustler, a real good man who could even spell. Just to prove it, he once published a boxing magazine called *Bang!*

When Borden started the magazine, he was living in Chicago and was afflicted by a terrible case of the shorts. He went to see Joe Glaser. In later years, Glaser became a successful manager of black orchestras and put Louis (Satchmo) Armstrong's name in lights on Broadway, but then he was a guy booking acts and managing fighters out of a two-room office in The Loop.

"I want to start a magazine," Borden told Glaser, "but I'm broke. I need a backer." Glaser offered to defray the costs and suggested that Borden use one of his two rooms as an editorial office. He even provided a typewriter.

On that typewriter, Borden wrote an editorial blasting Glaser as a "front" for Al Capone in the management of fighters. Borden took the suggestion that he get out of town.

That was Eddie Borden. I said he could spell; he could. His trouble was that he knew the difference between principle and principal. Not many people in boxing can make the same claim.

Borden was a gambler. He would bet on anything, like how many minutes it would take him to run around a block or how many honest men there were in Wall Street. He could name the casts of Broadway plays going back many years and if you doubted him, he would lay a price on his memory. He wore glasses and looked like a college prof, but Broadway was his campus.

One afternoon Borden was arrested in Yankee Stadium for betting on baseball. The unfortunate blow struck while Borden was seated in the bleachers just below a huge sign warn-

2

ing the customers that betting was prohibited. The cops took Borden in and a magistrate set bail at $50. Hard luck sometimes brings people together, but not when one is a broken bettor and the other is a magistrate. Borden found himself in the lockup. He was allowed to use a phone to get word downtown that he was in stir.

Within hours a turnkey told Borden, "There's a guy out here to go your bail."

"Who is he?"

"Who knows? Says he's a friend of yours."

Borden walked from the lockup toward the police sergeant's desk. There was Walker waving a $50 bill under the sergeant's nose. "You?" Borden screamed. He started back toward the lockup, turned to confront Walker and shouted, "I wouldn't let you bail me out if I was in for murder." Then, turning once again, he walked right back into the lockup.

That is the kind of guy Borden was, which brings me back to what I was saying in the beginning. There are guys in boxing you cannot budge with a trip hammer if they think they are right. Not with a trip hammer; money is another story. Borden was different by inclination. He never took a marker on his honor.

When World War II broke out in September 1939, he went up to Canada to enlist in the Canadian Army. Everybody thought he was nuts and some said he was in dire straits, up to his neck in hock to shylocks. When the war ended, Borden was mustered out in London, where he began making book.

One day I got a call from him. A fight was coming up in London between Bruce Woodcock and Lee Oma. Woodcock was a Yorkshire heavyweight who had a punch and two left feet. Oma was out of Detroit. He had all the moves, but he could not punch. He was good enough to outbox most anybody if he wanted to, which he often did not. When his fighting days were over, he wound up tending bar, which surprised nobody intimately acquainted with his history. He was the only fighter I ever knew who could handle a drink with boxing gloves on. But he was a hell of a boxer.

"Who do you like between Woodcock and Oma?" Borden asked on the phone.

"Woodcock," I said.

"You're nuts," Borden said. "This Limey won't lay a glove on Oma."

"I'm telling you Woodcock," I insisted.

"You don't know what you're talking about. Oma's the favorite here."

"Then bet Oma," I said. I was mad. "All I know, I saw him yesterday and asked him how he felt. No good, he said. When Lee Oma says he ain't feeling good, bet against him."

Oma went to London and got knocked out in the fourth round. The fight was so bad, it raised a stink. Peter Wilson was the best boxing writer in England and the headline on his story in *The Daily Mirror* said, "Oma! Aroma! Coma!" The British Boxing Board of Control held up Oma's purse. I don't know if he ever got paid. Borden blew a bundle. When he thought he was right, nothing would change his mind, not even a water job.

What I know is that when a fighter says he doesn't feel good, start smelling around for a fish on the floor. I had one rule when I was running boxing in Madison Square Garden. I never forced a fighter to go through with a bout if he said he was under the weather.

The night of Sonny Liston's second bout with Muhammad Ali, the one they moved to Lewiston, Maine, because Liston had mob connections, I walked into his dressing room with Joe Louis. Louis patted Sonny on the back and said, "Good luck, Sonny."

Liston looked him straight in the eye. He said, "Joe, I don't feel so good."

4

"What do you mean you don't feel so good? You gonna win," Louis said.

Liston looked down. When he raised his head he said, "Just ain't right, Joe," Then he went out and we went back to our seats, and I kept thinking of the way Liston acted. We were back in our seats a few minutes when the fight started and Ali went into his shuffle. Liston flicked a couple of jabs at Ali but they missed. I saw Ali throw a long right, while he was up on his toes, and it glanced off Liston's jaw. He went down.

Jersey Joe Walcott was the referee. He was the heavyweight champion until Rocky Marciano hit him on the chin one night in Philadelphia. Now, working the fight, he was so flustered when Liston hit the floor, he wasted maybe twenty seconds before starting the count.

Liston wasn't moving and finally Walcott counted him out. The fight was over. The crowd was stunned. Geez, I thought, Liston was trying to tell Louis something in the dressing room. The official time was one minute of the first round. Along the way somebody lost forty seconds or so. Liston must have been down for twenty seconds. The crowd didn't like anything about the short fight. The place in which the fight was held was a small joint, and the booing bounced off the walls. Sounded like a rumble of thunder. Liston stamped around the ring, insisting he beat the count. He had not been hit hard enough to be knocked off his feet.

I kept thinking of the first one between Ali and Liston, the one in Miami Beach, when Liston quit in his corner after the sixth round. Claimed he injured his left shoulder. Maybe. All I remembered was that when the fight was over and Ali was the new world heavyweight champion, I went into Liston's dressing room and waited for him to come back from the ring.

The moment Liston came through the door he reached down with his left hand and picked up an armchair and threw it

5

across the room. Must have weighed fifty pounds. Made a terrible racket when it hit the wall. "Motherfucker!" Liston screamed. The sound of his voice was sharper than the chair smashing against the wall. His rage filled the room and suddenly it seemed crowded, though only a few of his handlers were with him. I walked out.

Outside, I was thinking, if Liston had thrown a punch as hard as he heaved the chair, maybe he would have kept the heavyweight title and the world would have been deprived of Ali's coronation.

Later, I heard that Liston threw both fights to Ali but I didn't believe it because there is one thing you can count on in boxing. If there are two ways to look at things, somebody sooner or later is going to come up with a dirty picture.

By the time Liston was found dead in his house in Las Vegas, five years after his second fight with Ali, the story went around that somebody had given him an overdose of drugs to get him out of the way. That one was hard to buy. One thing I knew about Liston was that he was in deadly fear of a needle. Wouldn't even let doctors shoot anything into him when he needed a shot for a bad hand or a cold.

The night before Liston's funeral, Louis was shooting crap in Caesar's Palace in Las Vegas with Abe Margolies. There is one thing you can be sure of. Louis was using Margolies's money. Abe was a rich manufacturer of jewelry in New York and a good friend of Louis. He liked to have Joe around and it was nothing for him to keep his friend heeled. That night the dice were cold for them. Margolies called it quits after midnight. He told Joe, "Meet me here tomorrow. Maybe we'll get lucky."

"Can't, Abe," Louis said. "Tomorrow's Liston's funeral and I'm a pallbearer."

"Too bad," Margolies said. "I was going to give you $5,000 to play with."

6

Louis's nice face cracked into a smile. He said, "Abe, maybe I can skip the funeral. Sonny would understand."

He went to the funeral anyway and helped carry Liston on his way. It was a matter of principle.

The Shirt Off My Back

I gave the shirt off my back to get into boxing. What I mean is that I went from selling shirts for a company on Fifth Avenue to selling left hooks. One thing I know, if a guy can sell one item, he can sell anything. Like when I was a kid, living in Brooklyn in an apartment in Borough Park, I used to sell newspapers on the subway.

It was not easy in those days, not for my family anyway. My father was a skilled cutter of leather for fine women's shoes and handbags, but it was the Great Depression which made things rough. We lived one step ahead of the landlord. What helped was that things were so tough, landlords had to give new tenants concessions, which meant the first two months you lived in a flat rent-free. After the first two months, you looked around for another apartment. We moved a lot.

I was going to James Madison High School in Brooklyn, but nights I made a few dollars selling newspapers. I sold the *American*, the *News*, and the *Mirror*. The *Times* and the *Herald-*

Tribune were too heavy. They were those regular-size eight-column papers and when you carried twenty-five or fifty of them you could hardly move. I sold tabloids. They did not weigh so much.

Like the *News*, which sold for two cents in those days. I'd get a nickel for it on the subway. I'd pick up the papers at the DeKalb Avenue station of the West End line and sell them on the train all the way to Coney Island. That was the end of the line, so I'd stay on the same train and ride back to DeKalb Avenue, still selling papers, and if I was lucky, I'd sell out.

It was swell when I did that. I'd buy fifty papers for 75 cents and at a nickel each I'd make $1.75 on the investment. I was the kind of kid who wouldn't take guff from anybody, but I wasn't a bad kid. I had ambition and what do you think my big ambition was? I wanted to get a spot on a street corner where I could sell my papers, instead of working the subway. When it happened, it was a big step up for me.

I was in the open and I got to know the people who bought my papers, and one of them was a gangster named Frankie Yale. He was a big shot who would give me 25 cents for a two-cent paper. He was the first mobster I ever knew. Later, in boxing, I got to know others.

The night I remember from the time I was selling papers was May 12, 1932. That night I sold a thousand copies of the *Daily News* and a thousand copies of the *Daily Mirror*. That was because the headline said: "Baby Dead!"—the Lindbergh baby, murdered by his kidnapper. It was a big story—sad, too—but what it meant to me was that I sold two thousand papers that night.

After a while I had no more time for selling papers. I was playing a lot of playground basketball and made the varsity team in James Madison High School. But in my senior year I quit school and got a job with a company selling women's corsets.

Now, when I think of it, it was funny, but in the Depression just having a job was a serious matter.

It was about this time that I really got interested in boxing. I started going to the Young Men's Hebrew Association—they called it the "Bensonhurst Y"—and that is where I met Irving Cohen. He was the boxing instructor there, but later he got his name in the papers a lot because he was the manager of Rocky Graziano and Billy Graham, and other real good fighters.

Dan Parker used to write that "butter wouldn't melt" in Irving Cohen's mouth. Parker was the sports editor of the *Daily Mirror* in New York, which died a few years ago. So did Parker. When he was writing, he was a real knocker. He kept boxing people on their toes, because he had more spies than the CIA. The informers got good treatment in his column. Irving was a problem for Parker. What can you say about a man who ran a lingerie shop and had a good family and spoke so softly, you had to listen carefully to get his words.

Though he had to deal with at least one gangster in boxing, Irving kept his name clean. Not even Parker went after him when it became public that he was associated with Eddie Coco in the management of Rocky Graziano.

Coco was a small man with a big reputation in the mob. He had a police record as long as your income tax form and some years ago he was convicted in Florida of shooting a man to death. Before Coco was sentenced to prison for a long term, Al Weill, who was Rocky Marciano's manager, wrote to the judge and said, "I've known Eddie Coco for twenty-five years and I've always found him to be a straight shooter." Could be the judge didn't have a sense of humor. He threw the book at Coco, and it wasn't *The Ring Record Book* either.

By the time Cohen became associated with Coco he had been in boxing for many years. His first fighter was Marty Pomerantz, but by the time I got to know him he was handling a welterweight named Eddie Alzek. I started to go around to boxing with Cohen. Monday nights it was the St. Nicholas Arena, Tuesday nights it was either the Bronx Coliseum or the Broadway Arena in Brooklyn. Madison Square Garden ran on Friday nights and on Saturday there were fights at the Ridgewood Grove on the Brooklyn-Queens borderline.

One night in 1938, I went over to Garfield, N.J., with Irving. He had Alzek working on percentage in an eight-round bout with Freddie (Red) Cochrane. Six years later, Cochrane won the world welterweight championship by upsetting Fritzie Zivic in fifteen rounds, but in 1938 he was just another fighter from Elizabeth, N.J.

The fight was held in an outdoor arena in Garfield, and because the weather was overcast, a small crowd paid their way in. While the fighters were still in their corners awaiting the opening bell, the referee came to Cochrane's corner and greeted Willie Gilzenberg, Cochrane's manager.

"What's in it for me?" the referee asked Gilzenberg, a hard-bitten man who was called "the Beard" because five minutes after he shaved, he looked as if he needed another shave.

"What's in it for you?" Gilzenberg snarled. "Look at the house. We're on a percentage and we'll be lucky to get peanuts. Go take a walk."

The referee scowled and turned away. Crossing the ring, he approached Cohen and repeated the question: "What's in it for me?"

Cohen turned his baby-blue eyes on the referee. He had the countenance of a cherub and when he was embarrassed his face assumed the form of a newborn infant whose bottom had been spanked for the first time. His eyes had the expression of scared rabbits.

"Aw, gee," Irving Cohen said, "look at the house. We're hardly going to make expenses. I'm sorry but there's nothing in it for you."

12

By now the referee realized that neither side was going to stake him. In New Jersey in those days, the decision in a fight was solely in the hands of the referee; there were no judges at ringside.

Alzek and Cochrane hit each other with everything but the referee's scorecard and when the fight was over, they were so tired they could hardly make their way to their corners. Alzek clearly deserved the decision.

Now it was time for the referee to announce his decision. He called both fighters to the center of the ring and just as calmly as a man sitting down to Sunday breakfast, he raised both of their hands. Both corners screamed, but the referee had the last laugh. "No tickee, no washee," I thought. Right then and there I decided that boxing was going to be my game. I had a vision of big things happening to me in it. As we drove back to Brooklyn, Irving said, "What a rotten game this is."

I Learn How to Use a Screwdriver

The Navy got me in World War II. That was their problem. I went into the Seabees and wound up in Honolulu. Immediately, the price on the Japanese went to 8 to 5. That wasn't too bad. I had a friend named Ash Resnick who became a captain in the Army. Phil Foster, the comedian from Brooklyn, said the Germans went to 2 to 1 when Ash got his commission.

There was no good reason for me to be in the Seabees. We went all over the Pacific building bases for the Navy. I couldn't build a doll house, but the Seabees took me anyway and I spent two and one-half years in Hawaii and Midway. If the Japanese had known, they never would have surrendered.

Once I got as far as New Guinea with the Seabees. We went there on an errand of mercy. The Army needed a new officers' club, so they sent us to New Guinea to build it. It was an experience I have not forgotten. How many people can say they went all the way to New Guinea to learn how to use a screwdriver?

When I got out of the Navy in 1946, I came home with nothing to do. It seemed everybody in the Service had learned to use a screwdriver. Jobs were scarce. My wife, Judy, was working and I had time to spend the afternoons in Stillman's Gym. What made it possible was the "52–20 Club" under the GI Bill of Rights. This was the Government's way of helping former GI's to get on their feet. We were guaranteed $20 a week for an entire year and in those days, like now, a year included fifty-two weeks.

I started to go to Stillman's Gym to kill time. Right from the start I was hooked. I liked to watch fighters working out, to smell the sweat and to see guys hitting other guys, some feeling good, others just snorting and slipping punches, slick with sweat and their veins bulging.

Any day there were a couple of hundred fighters and managers hanging around the gym, which was on Eighth Avenue, between 54th and 55th streets, four blocks from the old Madison Square Garden. It was run by a guy whose real name was Lou Ingber, only he was called Lou Stillman.

Actually, the place got its name from Marshall Stillman. Few remember him now, but he was a millionaire swell who had an idea he could do good by opening a gym for tough guys. He believed that if they were taught to box, they would not go around putting knives into people or shooting bullets at nice little old ladies. They did not call it mugging in those days, but that was the kind of thing Marshall Stillman had in mind. He said it gave New York a bad name. He was ahead of his time.

When he opened the gym he put Lou Ingber in charge, because he thought the guy could handle the action. Ingber had been a private detective who wore a gun like he wore his pants. Carried it with him all the time, even when he quit being a private eye. He was a strange man who could fart in public and then go home and paint in oils. Just why he wore the gun I do not know, because there were no gangsters in the gym, not every day anyway.

By the time I started hanging around, Marshall Stillman was dead and the guy who took his last name owned the joint. What I remember about it is that Lou Stillman had two signs posted. One said, "Wash Your Dirty Clothes!" The other warned, "Anyone Caught Stealing Will Be Barred For Life!" Stillman must have been a lousy detective or they had very good crooks in the gym. Nobody ever got barred.

Stillman ran the place from a high stool near two rings on the main floor of the gym. That was his office. A wall clock above him timed the rounds and there was a mike on a shelf by his shoulders. Believe me when I tell you he did not need the mike. He had a voice you could hear above the crowd in Times Square on New Year's Eve. Stillman treated all fighters the same way—nasty. He always said, "Treat them right and they'll eat you alive." Nobody ever put the bite on him.

Managers and matchmakers did their business in this smoke-filled slum. Managers talked while their fighters quietly took their lumps. The building that housed it has been replaced by a twenty-story apartment house. When I walk by it now I think of the way it was. And I think of Irving Cohen. Just like flowers grow out of manure, Irving bloomed in that unsanitary dump.

Iriving Cohen was a dead honest guy, which, for me, he proved when he was managing Billy Graham. In 1951, Graham was signed to fight Kid Gavilan for the world welterweight championship in Madison Square Garden. A few days before the fight, Irving got word that Frankie Carbo wanted to see him. When Carbo called, people answered. He was described by the newspapers as the underworld's overlord of boxing.

I said Irving was honest; I didn't say he was brave or fool-

17

ish. He went to see Carbo at the bar in the old Forrest Hotel on 49th Street, down the block from the Garden.

"You want your boy should be the champ?" Carbo said.

"Sure, of course," Irving said. "That's what he's fighting Gavilan for."

"You give me twenty percent of him and you get the title," Carbo said.

Irving's baby-blue eyes got old suddenly. "Frank, I can't give you twenty percent," the manager said. "I got a piece and there's Jack Reilly, who brought Billy to me. He's got a piece. There ain't room for you."

Carbo said, "Talk to the fighter. He's the one that's got the say."

So Irving talked to Graham and Graham didn't go for it. "Listen, if I have to turn on my friend Reilly I'd rather not have the title," the fighter said. "A guy wants to be champ, but he don't have to be a louse to get it."

Billy Graham was that kind. In fifteen years he had 126 fights and was never off his feet. Everybody knew he was a professional, an artist in the trade, and he could do more with gloves on than anybody, maybe up to Sugar Ray Robinson. I used to tell Billy, "You're such a good boxer, you always make it look easy. That's why you don't excite people."

When Cohen told Carbo there was no deal, Carbo said, "Does the kid know he ain't going to win?" "He knows," Irving said. "He's got a lot to learn about life," Carbo said.

In two fights before their title bout, Graham won the first, Gavilan the second. Gavilan was a flashy puncher. He grew up in Cuba and learned a "bolo" punch, which was really an uppercut. Graham was a New York kid, an East Sider who had all the moves, which he got as a kid at the Catholic Boys' Club on the East Side of Manhattan.

The title fight with Gavilan went fifteen rounds, all of

them close, and when it was over, I had Billy the winner. What Graham did was to wait for Gavilan's leads and if it was a jab he would pick it off. What he could always do was to turn from the other guy's rights and step inside the long punches. He won it ten rounds to five, but as Johnny Addie announced the decision a great roar came down from the balconies. The people were angry and around ringside the big spenders were screaming at the officials.

In New York State referees and judges use both round-by-round scoring and point scoring. If a fight ends with both fighters having scored the same number of rounds, then points count. The points are scored on a scale of one to four in each round.

The referee, Mark Conn, had it seven rounds for Graham, seven rounds for Gavilan, with one even, but gave the decision to Gavilan, ten points to seven. One of the two judges, Frank Forbes, had the same round score, but voted for Graham, eleven points to ten. The second judge, Artie Schwartz, called it nine rounds for Gavilan to six for Graham. Gavilan got a split decision.

I remember the way Graham stood in the center of the ring, dumbfounded as his supporters came out of their seats into the aisles, waving their fists toward the ring, screaming threats at Conn and Schwartz. Security men kept the angry crowd from storming the ring.

What else I remember is what Irving Cohen told me about Artie Schwartz, the judge who had a lopsided card in favor of Gavilan. Many years later, as Schwartz lay dying in a New York hospital, he sent a message to Irving to come and see him. When Irving went into the hospital room, he wished Schwartz well, which was like Irving. He was the softest, kindest man I ever knew.

Irving said Schwartz looked up at him from his bed and said, "You know, Irving, I got to get this off my mind because you are a very decent fellow. When I voted for Gavilan against Graham I had to do it. I want you to know this. The boys ordered me to do it. I couldn't help myself and it's bothered me ever since. I'm sorry, Irving, for what I did to you and Graham."

When Irving told me the story later, he said, "Poor guy. I know what he meant. The boys order you to do something, you do it, if you want to live. At least Schwartz got it off his chest. He died in peace, I hope."

4

Matchmaker, Matchmaker, Make Me a Match

Two years before Graham got robbed in the Garden, I went to work there as the assistant matchmaker. Al Weill was the matchmaker, working for Jim Norris's International Boxing Club, and the year was 1949. I was hired to assist Weill in making matches for the Garden and to be the matchmaker at the St. Nicholas Arena, which the Garden had leased to make sure it had a place to run shows in on the nights the Garden was occupied by other events.

What made this necessary was television. Boxing was a big thing on television and the Garden had contracts with the razorblade people and the beer people to put shows on TV, and that's why they had the St. Nicholas Arena as well as the Garden. Everybody called the place St. Nick's and it was known as one of the best neighborhood boxing clubs in the business.

One day I got a phone call from Weill. He said he was home and wasn't coming to the office, and would I make the matches for the next couple of weeks. The real story was that

Weill was having trouble with the tough guys. They wanted him to make matches he objected to. So he was disgusted and when he called me, he said, "Teddy, I'm sick. I'm not coming in. Take my salary. Do anything you want. I don't want my salary. Just put the shows in."

"You're the boss," I said, and I went around and made a lot of matches, real good ones. In my whole career as a matchmaker I never made a match I didn't believe in except one, which I will tell you about later. I had one theory. The people pay to see a fight and should get their money's worth. The only way to give them their money's worth was to put in tough matches.

Weill wasn't that kind of matchmaker. He was a boxing politician who held hands with the mob. And he owned his own fighters. I didn't. In forty years in the game I never managed a fighter or had a piece of another manager's fighter. Weill didn't work that way. He had pieces of fighters and even owned Rocky Marciano, who became the world heavyweight champion. But I was just a matchmaker. That's all I ever wanted to be.

Go into any town in America where they have boxing and it's a good bet you will find the matchmaker is the most unpopular man in town. Fight managers hate matchmakers. They think their fighters belong on every card. The way I figure, if a matchmaker makes a match, it should be the kind of fight he would pay money to see himself, between the two best fighters available.

While I was working with Weill I had the responsibility of making the preliminary bouts in the Garden. Weill was on my ass a lot because I wouldn't listen to him. One time he came to me and suggested that I use a fighter named Charley Norkus in a semi-final in the Garden. Norkus was from New Jersey and was a good puncher, a heavyweight.

What I knew about Norkus was that Weill had a piece of him. Norkus was managed by a Jersey guy named Abe Bressler, who had trouble moving the fighter before he put Weill in for a

22

piece of the action. I put Norkus in with Curt Kennedy in a Garden semi-final of ten rounds. Kennedy was an Irishman with Indian blood from Wichita, Kansas, who had a lot of Amateur Athletic Union titles and won eighteen of his first twenty bouts when he turned pro.

When I made the match I wondered why Weill let Norkus fight Kennedy. When I saw them in the ring together I was still wondering. The fight was so one-sided, Kennedy won every round on the cards of the three officials. And when it was over I thought, well, we got rid of Norkus. Weill won't let him fight Kennedy again.

Now I had a match scheduled in the St. Nicholas Arena on the Gillette Cavalcade of Sports, between Archie Moore and Jimmy Bivins. They were real good fighters. Moore had been active since 1936 and later won the world light-heavyweight championship from Joey Maxim. But in 1950, the time I'm talking about, he couldn't get himself arrested in New York.

Would you believe that this great fighter had only two fights in fourteen years in New York? So I put him in with Bivins at the St. Nick's, knowing it would be a hell of a match because Bivins had a reputation as a guy with a punch who still could flatten an opponent if he hit him right.

When you stop to think of such a match being made for a neighborhood fight club you have to wonder. These days fighters of Moore's and Bivins's ability get millions of dollars to fight on TV. We'll never know, but it is my idea that Moore or Bivins could beat people like Larry Holmes or Ken Norton like breaking sticks. Years later, Moore gave Marciano one of his hardest fights and this was when Moore had been fighting for nineteen years and was forty-three years old.

I got word one day that Bivins had been hurt while train ing—a bad hand or something—and would not be able to keep his date with Moore. It was difficult to get a substitute for Bivins because nobody wanted to fight Moore, he was so good.

23

When Weill heard about my problem with the St. Nick's fight, he kept bugging me every day, asking, "Teddy, what did you do for that St. Nick's date?" and I always said, "I'll get somebody for Archie Moore, you can depend on that."

Finally, Weill said to me, "Teddy, why don't you forget Moore and fill that St. Nick date with a return between Kennedy and Norkus?"

I said, "Al, are you crazy? They fought. The three officials voted all ten rounds in favor of Kennedy. There's no way that they are going to fight again, not while I'm making matches for the St. Nick's."

"Well, Jim likes the match," Weill said.

"I know Jim Norris is the boss of the International Boxing Club," I said, "but if he likes the match he better come in here and tell me how much he likes it, because I have no intention of putting it in."

I worked hard looking for an opponent for Moore, somebody who could fill in for Bivins. I finally got a guy by the name of Sid Peaks to substitute against Moore, but he got hurt in a fight and had to pull out. I was stuck and time was growing short. "Why don't you do like I say?" Weill said, "Jim would like to see Norkus and Kennedy in there."

I knew Weill had a piece of Norkus, which was not allowed by New York State law, but I couldn't tell it to him to his face. After all, he was my boss. I was only the assistant matchmaker. He kept repeating, "Y'know, Jim would like to see you do it. He's not going to ask you, but he'd like it."

So I said, "All right, I'll ask Jim." I walked into Norris's office and I said, "Jim, Weill keeps telling me you'd like me to put Norkus and Kennedy in the St. Nick's. I don't see any reason for them to fight. It was a no-contest fight the first time, Kennedy won every round. Do you really want that fight?"

24

83
1510

Norris said, "Well, if you can do it without hurting anybody I'd like to see that fight again." I made the rematch.

The night of the fight, Irving Brown came to me at St. Nick's. He said, "Teddy, I want to talk to you." He was a guy I knew, a brother of Freddie Brown, the fight trainer who is still around, working with Roberto Duran and people like that.

I said to Irving Brown, "What do you want to talk to me about?"

"There's something wrong with this fight," he said. "Do you know what it is?"

Irving Brown was a gambler. He is dead now, but when he was around, he knew as much about boxing as anybody, which is to say he knew all the angles. If a fight was in the bag, Irving Brown got the word. He wasn't fooled easily. So when he told me there was something wrong with the return match between Kennedy and Norkus, I listened carefully.

"Who do you think is going to win?" Brown asked.

I said, "Kennedy licked him ten out of ten rounds the first time they fought. There's no reason he won't lick him again."

He said, "Would you bet even money on the fight?"

I said, "Are you crazy? Of course I would," and Irving Brown said, "All right, you've got a $200 bet on Norkus. You don't have to pay if you lose." He looked me straight in the eyes. "I think there's something wrong with this fight, but you don't have to pay me on the bet if you lose."

He walked away, but ten minutes later he was back. "You have another $200 bet on Norkus but you don't have to pay if Kennedy gets knocked out."

Now I was angry. I looked at Irving Brown and I said, "Why, you crazy son of a bitch, Kennedy ain't going to get licked."

"There's something wrong with this fight," Brown said.

25

"I smell it. Everybody up in the balcony is looking to bet that Kennedy gets knocked out, at any price. Don't you think there's something wrong?"

Now I started thinking. What I thought about was Al Weill. I was beginning to get suspicious. "Could be," I said to Brown. I ran over to a member of the New York State Athletic Commission, a guy named Dan Dowd. They used to call him "Baldy" because he had no hair. He had a lot to learn about boxing. He got the job because he was in the district attorney's office and somebody came up with the bright idea that if he was in the D.A.'s office, he would be a good man to keep the boys in boxing honest. Fat chance.

I told Dowd, "Dan, there's something wrong with this fight. I hear Norkus can't lose. Kennedy is going into the water."

Once a cop, always a cop. "What proof do you have?" Dowd said.

"No proof," I said, "except that certain people tell me everybody's looking to bet on Norkus."

"That's no proof," Dowd said. "But I'll tell you what I'm going to do. I'll look at the fight very carefully."

"Okay," I told Dowd. "You make sure, because if there's anything wrong, between rounds you better let them know that they won't get paid if it's a fake."

When Norkus and Kennedy came to the center after the opening bell, Norkus threw two left jabs. Both missed. A third jab landed on Kennedy's chin. He went down and was counted out. The crowd started to boo. I ran down to Dowd and I said, "I told you there was something wrong with the fight," and he looked up at me from his seat and said, "The punch looked perfectly good to me." He gave no importance to anything I said to him and I said plenty.

The next day I went to the boxing department in the Garden—the offices of the International Boxing Club. It was a

Saturday, but we were open because in those days we used to pay the fighters the morning after a fight. Al Weill was in when I got there, and I asked him to come into my office.

When Weill came in, he looked over at a little old gray-haired guy who seemed to be asleep in a chair. His name was Phil Lewis, only he was called "Razor Phil" because he had been known to cut the faces of people with whom he was trying to make a point. He was a funny little hustler who sold tickets twice a year to an annual testimonial dinner to himself.

When Weill walked into my office, I grabbed him by the throat and I kept banging his head against the wall, screaming, "You son of a bitch, you set the thing up. You know if anything happened, an investigation or anything, I'd be the fall guy, I wouldn't work with you another day."

Harry Markson heard the noise and came running into my office. He was the director of boxing for IBC, a good man with decent instincts. He should have taught English in a college, but he got into the boxing business because he was a newspaperman. He had class.

"Stop it, stop it, Teddy," Markson said, trying to pull me off.

I wouldn't let go of Weill. And I kept screaming, saying, "I don't want to work in this fucking place. I won't work for Al Weill. You tell Jim Norris that if he wants me to work for the IBC he's got to fire Weill. If he doesn't fire Weill I quit."

By this time Weill's face was turning blue. I released my grip on him and he ran out of my office, trailed by Markson. I was alone, except for "Razor Phil" Lewis, who got up out of the chair in which he was faking sleep. Straightening his clothes, and rising to his full five feet, Razor Phil said to me, "You should have killed the son of a bitch, sonny."

The next week I went into Jim Norris's office to see the boss. "Why don't you calm down, Teddy," Norris said. "It was

27

just one of those things, y'know. Everybody says it was a good punch, a knockout punch." I said, "Jim, I don't give a shit what everybody says. I don't think it was a good punch and I quit."

I walked out of the joint and I never went back while Norris was running boxing in the Garden. Curt Kennedy was managed by Frank (Blinky) Palermo, the mobster who arranged Jake LaMotta's dump to Billy Fox in Madison Square Garden in 1947.

Ryan Stopped at Eboli

The hoodlums controlled boxing while Norris controlled Madison Square Garden. He walked with them and talked with them, and his matchmakers, first Al Weill and then Billy Brown, had to deal with Frankie Carbo. Carbo was not the only mobster in the game, but he was the biggest. I never really got to know him before the Feds put him in prison for eighteen years for conspiring to extort money from the manager of Don Jordan, who was the world welterweight champion from 1958 to 1960. I knew some of the hoodlums in boxing but I never got real close to any of them.

It wasn't easy doing business without getting involved with the mobsters, in one way or another. Carbo had his fingers on the throat of boxing and could squeeze the air out of it any time he wanted to make a move. If he did not own a certain fighter, he "owned" the manager. When Weill was Marciano's manager, he was controlled by Carbo. So was Felix Bocchicchio, who managed Jersey Joe Walcott, another heavyweight champion.

The hoodlums never bothered me. Once, when I was making the matches for Norris at St. Nick's, I tried to make a fight between Billy Graham and Tony Pellone, another New York welterweight from Greenwich Village. They had boxed twice before and Pellone won both times, but it was still a hot match and I went after it.

I knew I would not have any trouble with Graham, because he was managed by Irving Cohen, but the other half of the match was a problem. Pellone's manager was Tommy Ryan, a mob guy whose real name was Thomas Eboli and who was a big man in his fraternity. In those days the New York State Athletic Commission gave licenses to just about anybody. If a guy could breathe, he got a license. Ryan was licensed as a manager and second, and everybody knew he was Pellone's manager.

I have to say here that Ryan treated Pellone pretty good. He gave the kid a clean deal when they split up purses. Pellone was an ordinary fighter who always made good fights, and that's why I wanted him back with Graham at St. Nick's. He came from a poor family of fourteen kids—twelve sons, two daughters—and his father ran a tight ship. The fighter was a tough kid.

A newspaperman named Bill Heinz once asked Pellone what he did with his money. "Whatever money I make," the fighter said, "I take home to my old man. At first I didn't make much, but I'd give it to my old man, and he'd give me five dollars out of it. Then the time I fought Bob Montgomery at the Garden I got $8,513 for my end. So I took it home and I give it to my old man, and he said to me in Italian, 'How you fixed?' and I said, 'I'm broke.' 'All right,' he said. 'Here.' He give me the thirteen dollars. I said, 'Hey, thirteen is unlucky. Give me fourteen dollars instead.' Then my old man said, 'No, give me one dollar back. That makes twelve.'"

This day I'm in Norris's office and Ryan comes in, and I say, "Tommy, let's make Graham and Pellone in the St. Nicholas

Arena." He says, "I'll give you my home number. Call me eight o'clock tonight."

I called him at eight and Ryan said, "I thought about it. No, I don't like the Graham fight. There's not enough money in it."

"I'll call you later," I said, figuring I could wear him down. He was right about the money involved in the fight. At the time we were paying main-event fighters only $1,500 out of the television fee, that's all. It wasn't much.

Anyway, at nine o'clock I called Ryan again. He told me, "Didn't I tell you I don't want the match?" I said, "I thought maybe you changed your mind." I called him at ten o'clock, eleven o'clock, midnight, one, two in the morning. Finally, at two in the morning, he said to me, "Listen, you son of a bitch, if you call me once more I'll kill you."

You know, I had never had any problems with Tommy Ryan and was not familiar with his standing in the Mafia. I didn't look up to him or fear him. He was just another manager as far as I was concerned. Well, the next day I'm in my office, which adjoined Norris's in the old Garden, the one on Eighth Avenue and 50th Street in Manhattan, and I see Ryan walk into Norris's office. So I follow him in and say, "Tommy, let's make Graham and Pellone."

He takes one look at me and says, "Listen, you mother, see this window here, if you ask me for that match one more time I'm going to throw you right through this window." It was a casement window and I walked up to it and, releasing the catch, opened it wide. "What do you want to break the glass for?" I said. "Let's make Graham and Pellone. It's a real good match.

Ryan didn't know how to take me. He had never been treated this way, not this big man in the Mafia. What he did was to laugh and say, "All right, you son of a bitch, Jim is here now and I'm gonna make the match with you. I know you're not going to lie, but you've got to promise me one thing." "What's that?" I said, and he said, "You got to tell me where Graham eats the day of the fight. When they weigh in at the Commission at twelve o'clock you have to tell me where Graham is going to have his steak."

"You got a deal," I said, and we shook hands. I knew Graham's habits and on the day of the fight, after the weigh-in at noon, Ryan came over to me and said, "Where does Graham eat?"

"He eats at his mother's house," I said. "She cooks his steak for him the day of the fight."

"You son of a bitch," Ryan said. He was angry. He pointed at me and said, "You better sit with me tonight." I usually sat at ringside, but this night I sat next to Ryan in the balcony at old St. Nick's. It was a hard fight and Graham got the decision when it was over. Ryan didn't beef. He didn't even call me a son of a bitch.

The mob guys moved pretty good in boxing. They moved in on fighters or bought pieces, and Ryan wound up with a pretty good middleweight out of Luzerne, Pa., named Rocky Castellani. Castellani won a lot of fights around New York and was a hot attraction. Weill knew this and made a match for Madison Square Garden between Castellani and Ernie Durando, a good puncher out of Bayonne, N.J.

Why Ryan took the match I'll never know, for everybody in boxing knew that Weill had a piece of Durando, who was a stablemate of Charley Norkus. Bressler, the manager, had given Weill pieces of both fighters.

When Castellani and Durando climbed through the ropes, Ryan was working in his fighter's corner. He looked over to the other side of the ring and saw Ray Miller, a former hard-hitting lightweight who was now a referee on the staff of the New York State Athletic Commission. He thought, Hey, I know

Miller. He's not going to do anything to hurt me. Ryan, after all, had developed sound ties with certain members of the New York Boxing Commission and usually came up with the close decisions for his fighters. Miller's role as referee did not give him any concern. Ryan was confident that his boy Castellani would outbox the harder-hitting Durando. He was wrong.

In the seventh round, Durando hit Castellani with so many punches, Miller stopped the fight and awarded it to Durando by a knockout. In a flash, Ryan rushed across the ring and, pinning the referee in a neutral corner, began throwing punches at him. Miller, who was twenty years older then Ryan, blocked most of the punches. He was an old pro.

Within seconds, Ryan was grabbed by security men who jumped into the ring. He was led away and escorted to Castellani's dressing room. Weill had to be the dumbest man in Madison Square Garden that night. After the fight he went to Castellani's dressing room to offer condolences to the beaten fighter and was in the room when Ryan entered.

Ryan rushed across the big dressing room and pinned Weill against a wall. He slapped him hard and Weill's glasses shattered on the floor. Weill went down and Ryan, his dark eyes full of fire, kicked him a couple of times. People jumped in and pulled Ryan away.

The next day Ryan came up to the IBC's offices in the Garden. Harry Markson was at his desk. "I wanna apologize," Ryan said. "I wanna tell Weill I'm sorry." Markson got up from his desk and said, "Tommy, you have exactly sixty seconds to get out of this building before I call the cops." Ryan said, "Oh, for Christ sake, Harry, I'm man enough to come in and apologize. Y'know I'm sorry. I lost my temper."

"You've got thirty seconds now," Markson said. He picked up the phone to call the security men in the Garden. Ryan turned and walked out. He never managed another fighter.

Ryan became a very big man in the mob, but he made the mistake of having a sweetheart in Brooklyn. One night his enemies waited for him to come out. They shot him through the head and stuffed his body into the trunk of his car, where it was discovered a few days later.

When Talking
Men Talked

When I walked out of the Garden after my trouble with Weill, I wasn't worried. I was confident that I could always make a living in boxing. By that time, Judy and I had a family. Our son, Richard, was eight years old, and our daughter, Marsha, was four. But it was like I always say, everything happens for the better. Because I really believe this, some people say I'm arrogant. Maybe so. It's no big deal. I just believe in myself. I don't care how people react to me. If I'm right, I take a stand and I stand on it. I felt I was right when I told Weill off. I'm the emotional type. When you've had as many ups and downs as I've had you get that way.

It wasn't the first time I left the Garden in a huff. In 1946, Nat Rogers, the matchmaker for Mike Jacobs's 20th Century Sporting Club, was suspended for a year by the New York Boxing Commission for doing business with unlicensed managers. Fellow named Chickie Bogard was made the matchmaker and I was brought in as his assistant.

Mike Jacobs wasn't active in the club because he had suffered a stroke. Sol Strauss, Jacobs's lawyer, was running the store, with Harry Markson working as the director of boxing. I got to tell you here about something they used to say about the 20th Century Sporting Club.

First I must let you know that Rogers, the matchmaker, wore glasses; Strauss, the lawyer, wore a hearing aid, and Jacobs, the promoter, wore false teeth that did not fit very good. What they used to say about the three was that Rogers took off his glasses to read, Strauss turned off his hearing aid to hear, and Jacobs took out his dental plates to eat. They were three of the funniest looking guys in boxing.

I worked for the 20th Century Sporting Club for one year and I tried my best to put good shows on. Bogard was a good guy to work with and Markson was a prince, and I worked hard to keep things going.

The managers loused up a nice situation. They formed the Boxing Managers' Guild and demanded a larger cut from the money Gillette paid for broadcasting rights. That was when we had the Gillette Cavalcade of Sports and there were fights in the Garden or St. Nick's every Friday night. Strauss would not settle with the Guild, but I went along making matches each week.

There's one thing about making boxing matches, everybody knows about them the minute they are made, because it is impossible to keep a secret in the game. Talking men talk. So every week I would make a match by signing guys like Major Jones, a fighter out of Kansas City who could not get much work because he was too black and too good. That's the way things were in those days. Or I would try to use another great black fighter who was called Bert Lytell, a southpaw who could knock your head off with one punch if you were stupid enough to get into the ring with him.

Each time I made a match, the Guild got wind of it and

before long I would get word that this or that fighter had hurt his head or his back in training and could not keep his date in the Garden. You'd have to be stupid not to know that there was something wrong, and what everybody knew was that Frankie Carbo was operating on the side of the Guild. Soon as he heard that I signed a fighter, he got word to the fighter's manager that it would be unwise, if not unsafe, to cooperate with the Garden. At the same time the Guild put out the word that any fighter who worked in the Garden would be boycotted in the future.

For the first time in years, the 20th Century Sporting Club could not deliver on its contract with Gillette. There was no boxing in the Garden for five straight weeks. Sol Strauss said to me, "If we don't run a show next week, you're not going to get paid." I said, "Sol, it's all right with me. No pay, no Brenner. Goodbye."

I left and within a few months I signed a lease to promote boxing across the Hudson in Newark, N.J., in a club called Laurel Gardens. The place was falling apart. Ten years before it had been a prosperous arena run by Willie Gilzenberg and Babe Culnan, a couple of guys who knew boxing like David Rockefeller knows money.

What happened was that Gilzenberg and Culnan had been feuding with the sports editors of a couple of New Jersey newspapers and could not get any publicity. So they pulled out of Laurel Gardens. I moved in. First thing I did was to go over to see Abe J. Greene, who was chairman of the New Jersey State Athletic Commission. I asked him if he would give me a license to promote if I could rent Laurel Gardens. The reason I did this was that Gilzenberg and Culnan were very strong with the politicians in New Jersey and I thought, hey, they might try to stop me from coming into their territory.

Greene stood up like a soldier. He said, "Teddy, you can

have a license but I want to warn you, if the fights you put into the club are one-sided or favor jobs, I'll kick you back across the river."

When I presented my first main event for Greene's approval, he almost blew his top. "Teddy, I know, because people have told me, that you wouldn't put a fighter in unless you thought he could fight, but I can't approve this fight," Greene said. "This match has an odor to it."

I wasn't surprised. What I had done was to sign a match between Tami Mauriello, a New York heavyweight who had almost flattened Joe Louis two years before, and Mike Jacobs, a New Jersey heavyweight who was black and not related to the promoter of the same name.

Jacobs had been knocked out three straight times in fights that year, but that didn't bother me because one of the fighters who knocked him out was Billy Fox, the Philadelphia light-heavyweight for whom Jake LaMotta had gone into the water the year before. You did not have to be smart to figure that one out.

I said to Greene, "Listen, Abe, I guarantee this is going to be one hell of a fight. Jacobs is all puffed up over the chance to fight Mauriello and Mauriello has gone way back since he fought Louis. I tell you it'll be a good fight."

"If it isn't," Greene warned me, "you're going to have a lot of trouble with me."

It turned out to be a hell of a fight. Mauriello had Jacobs down five times in the first two rounds, but the referee let it continue. By the ninth round, Jacobs had control of the fight. He floored Mauriello in the last two rounds and when the final bell sounded, the customers were standing on their chairs, whistling and cheering. Mauriello got the decision, but Jacobs had saved my license.

"You can promote in New Jersey as long as you want to," the commissioner said. "Whatever fight you put in is good enough for me."

Greene was the best boxing commissioner I ever met. He was a newspaperman who ran the *Paterson Evening News* in New Jersey. Before that he had been a sportswriter and he loved boxing. By the time he became commissioner, he knew enough about the game to play it cool in any situation.

In 1950, Sugar Ray Robinson agreed to defend his welterweight title in a bout in Roosevelt Stadium, Jersey City, against Charley Fusari. The only reason the fight took place was that it was a benefit for the Damon Runyon Cancer Fund. Walter Winchell was head of the fund and he had enough influence then to get Robinson to agree to the fight.

All Robinson got for taking on Fusari was $5,000 to cover his training expenses, which was a very unusual thing for Sugar Ray. He was a fellow who made life difficult for promoters because he believed in getting well paid for his services. But he was also a soft touch when it came to helping out a good cause, and there was no better cause around than the Damon Runyon Cancer Fund.

The trouble was that Robinson could no longer make the welterweight limit of 147 pounds. He was fighting middleweights mostly and within six months would win the 160-pound title by knocking out Jake LaMotta in thirteen rounds. Making 147 pounds was an ordeal he could not survive.

That's where Abe Greene came in. Instead of insisting that Robinson weigh in at the same time as Fusari, who was a natural 147-pounder, he allowed Robinson to step on the scale in another room at another time on the day of the fight. No boxing writers were present. All they told them was that Robinson had weighed exactly 147 pounds. They took Abe Greene's word for it.

Fusari was managed by Vic Marsillo. He was a funny man. He once ran a radio talk show out of Jack Dempsey's restaurant on Broadway. One of his guests was a fight manager. Marsillo introduced the manager and then said to him, "Let's reminisce about next Friday night's Garden fight." But he was a realist. He had mob connections and was involved with Felix Bocchicchio, who had a criminal record as long as your arm and was the manager of Jersey Joe Walcott. He knew Fusari's limitations and when he accepted the bout with Robinson, he suggested that maybe it would be nice if Sugar Ray just went along for a gag.

So on the night of the fight, Robinson came out moving and Fusari, intent on winning the title, went after him with his best punches. Nobody was a better defensive fighter than Robinson. He could avoid punches by moving inside or out, or side to side, and he put on a hell of a show against Fusari, taking him along for the distance and getting the decision. The next day a boxing writer had it in his paper that Sugar Ray Robinson was the best carrier since Mother Dionne. Or was it Typhoid Mary?

What was funny about the whole thing was that at the end of the sixth round, Fusari came back to his corner and said to Marsillo, "I think I got this sucker figured out now. I'm going to open up in the next round and knock him out." Marsillo said, "Forget it. You're doing just fine. Just go out and box. We'll get the decision." He was worried that if Robinson was pressed, he would let fly with his sharp punches and flatten Fusari.

It was no disgrace to lose to Robinson, because pound for pound he was the greatest fighter I ever saw in the ring. A few months after he played with Fusari, he went to Europe and fought five fights in eight weeks. He knocked out four of his opponents. The way things are in boxing now, if a fighter has one fight in three months, he is a very busy fellow and people start worrying about his health.

Promoters and matchmakers said Robinson was tough to do business with, and they were mostly right. But nobody is one-way. He could do nice things, and if anybody wants any testimony to that, I will take an oath as a witness.

In 1950, when I almost choked Weill to death and walked away from Madison Square Garden for the second time, I ran a club called the Coney Island Velodrome. It was an old outdoor arena in which they ran bicycle races for many years. Now it was going to be torn down and I had one more show to put in the place. I went to Robinson and asked him if he would fight for me for a $1,000 purse.

"You're kiddin'," he said. "I just got $57,000 to fight Kid Gavilan, what can I get fighting in Coney Island?"

"It's for the Sports Lodge of B'nai B'rith," I said. "It's a new lodge and it needs to get started, and I thought I could put you in Coney Island and make some money for the lodge."

"That's asking a lot," Robinson said.

"You know, Max Kase is the president of the lodge and he's the sports editor of the *New York Journal-American*. It wouldn't hurt you with him if you agreed to fight on the benefit show."

Robinson thought about it and said, "Teddy, go out and see how much money you can get for me and then we'll talk about it."

I went to a radio station in Philadelphia that used to broadcast fights on Monday nights and I told the boss there I could get Sugar Ray for him, would he be interested. "We'll give you $750 for the rights," he said, "providing the fight goes at least four rounds, so we can get enough commercials in to break even."

"Is that all?" I said. "How can I offer that to Sugar Ray Robinson?"

"It's all we can afford," the radio guy said. So I said it was all right, that I would talk to Robinson about taking the guy he was fighting for at least four rounds.

Now I have to get an opponent for him and I hit on a welterweight named Billy Brown. He was not a top-notcher, but he could box real good, in the style of a Lee Oma, who could slip and slide and stay out of trouble if he was boxing on the level. Brown accepted the match.

George Gainford was Robinson's manager, He was a tall black guy with a deep voice who could strut like an emperor. He was mostly Robinson's trainer, but he had brought Sugar Ray up from the amateurs and acted as a kind of manager. Just to prove how smart Gainford was, he was the fellow who brought Gainford's Law into boxing, which says, "It didn't count how many seats you got in a theatre or arena. What counts is how many asses you got in them chairs."

I said to Gainford, "Do you think this Billy Brown can go four rounds with Sugar Ray? It's the only way we're going to get that $750 from the radio station."

Gainford pulled himself up to full height. He said, in his booming voice, "If it's four you want, four you'll get. Man, it'll go four."

The night of the fight it turned real cold. It was September, around Labor Day, and the wind came off the Atlantic Ocean at Coney Island. Robinson moved around to keep warm and tried to get Brown out of there as fast as he could so that he could shower and dress and get warm. But Brown kept moving and Robinson couldn't catch him. He couldn't get warmed up. The fight went the distance and Robinson got the decision. When I paid him $750 from the radio stations, plus the $1,000 purse, he didn't beef.

Fighters are funny. After Robinson lost the title to Carmen Basilio in Yankee Stadium, they fought again in the Chicago Stadium and this time Robinson got the middleweight title back. Both fights were wars and everybody knew a third fight would draw a big gate. Robinson, as the champ, stood to get a hell of a purse.

It was 1959 and both Robinson and Basilio were slightly past their primes. But Basilio wanted 30 percent of the gate and would not budge an inch. I was back in the Garden for the third time and I spoke to Sugar Ray. "Take it, It's the best match for you. You can get good money and you know Basilio. You fought him twice and you didn't get hurt. At this stage in your career where you going to go?"

One day I went up to Harlem to see Sugar Ray. I wasn't alone. Harry Markson was with me, and so were Ned Irish, the president of the Garden, and Admiral John J. Bergen, who was chairman of the board of the Garden. We met Robinson in his office on Seventh Avenue, a few doors up from the bar he owned.

First, Admiral Bergen presented Sugar Ray with a set of matched golf clubs. They had played together in Las Vegas and Bergen got to like Robinson, and so he gave him the clubs to show his appreciation. But then we started to talk business, and when one of us—I forget which one—offered Robinson half a million to fight Basilio, he thought for a minute and then said, "No, no, no. I can get more money than that."

Admiral Bergen stood up and said, "Ray, by God, I want to tell you something. You don't have anything to sell such as automobiles, clothing, or anything else. The only thing you have to sell of real value is Sugar Ray Robinson. By God, young man, if you can get more than $500,000 for a fight for Sugar Ray Robinson, then by all means go right ahead."

We all shook hands with Robinson and left, and we could not figure out where Robinson could get more than $500,000 for a fight. Later I got wind of the proposition Robinson had in mind. It came from a closed-circuit-television man named Irving Kahn who was new in boxing.

Sugar Ray was a pretty crafty guy and one night he invited Archie Moore to his house for dinner. Moore was still the world light-heavyweight champion, but it was late in his career. After twenty-three years in the ring, he was ready for the cleaners.

Robinson's wife, Edna Mae, cooked up a storm for Moore

and his wife that night. It was what is called a very genial dinner party and after they were finished, Sugar Ray said to Moore, "Archie, I'm going to make you more money than you ever made for a fight in your entire career—$250,000!"

"Well, that's great," Moore said. "Who do I have to fight, the Russian army?"

"No, you fight me," Robinson said.

"And how much you going to get?" Moore asked.

"I'm going to get $750,000. We're going to go on closed-circuit TV and sell out a lot of theatres, and we'll get rich."

Moore laughed and said, "Ray, you must think I'm the biggest chump of all time. You're going to get a shot at my title and take $750,000 for it, and I'm going to put my title up for $250,000. Man, that's great. Good night."

The fight never took place, of course, and Sugar Ray, who turned down $500,000 to defend the middleweight title against Basilio, lost it to Paul Pender in Boston for only $100,000. Whenever I see Robinson in California now, he laughs about the way things worked out for him. When he gets serious, he admits that he made a mistake. I think he still has the golf clubs Admiral Bergen gave him.

7

House of Upsets

It isn't easy to be a matchmaker. If a fight you put in is good, the fighters get the credit. If it is bad, the matchmaker gets the blame. The way I work is to try to get managers to put their fighters in with worthy opposition. It is not enough to put No. 1 in with No. 2. Anybody can do that. What you want is to blend styles, like putting in a boxer with a puncher. Then I have to decide whether it's a fight the fans want.

Long ago I said it like this. Take two fighters. One brings in the fans. The other brings his lunch in a paper bag. So I don't use the second fighter, and people say I'm playing favorites. When I was in the Garden that's what they said about Emile Griffith. They said I had a piece of him. That was a lie. I've never accepted a penny from anybody.

It's a no-win situation. In 1952, I went into the Eastern Parkway Arena in Brooklyn. The club was owned by Emile Lence, a nice little man who was in the garment business. He had a television contract with the Dumont network. It was for four weeks, with a seven-day cancellation clause. We ran 156 straight shows, every Monday night, and that was remarkable because Jim Norris's International Boxing Club had television shows on NBC-TV and CBS-TV every Friday and Wednesday nights, and we were competing with them for talent.

Eastern Parkway got to be known as "The House of Upsets" because underdogs won so many fights there. This made people say that I looked for those matches to bet on the underdogs. Not true. I'm a bettor, sure, but I bet only on football and baseball mostly. When I bet on a fight, it's a fight I had nothing to do with. That's a rule with me. All I ever wanted in this game was to put on the best fights I could make.

I started a lot of fighters off at Eastern Parkway who became world champions later, people like Floyd Patterson, who won the heavyweight title, and Gene Fullmer, who won the middleweight title. Patterson had twelve of his first twenty-one professional fights at the club, and this was a remarkable thing because the most money we could take in at the door was only $16,000.

What we would do was use most of the $16,000 to pay the fighters on the card. Lence's profit came out of the $8,000 we got from the Dumont network for each show. Eastern Parkway made more money in my three years there than many big arenas. It was only a small place. Once it had been a garage, but by the time Lence took it over it had been converted to a skating rink and, later, a bingo parlor. It became the greatest little fight club in America, The House of Upsets.

Patterson's first defeat happened at Eastern Parkway, in his fourteenth fight. I thought he beat Joey Maxim that night, but the officials voted for Maxim. I remember Arthur Susskind after the fight. He had boxed under the name of Young Otto, and people said he was one of the hardest punchers they had ever seen. But now, when Patterson lost to Maxim, Susskind was a boxing judge who had worked the fight and voted for Maxim.

When I saw him after the fight, I said, "Arthur, how could you give Patterson only one round?" He looked at me and said, "Oh, did I give him one round? I wonder how I came to do that. I don't think he even won a round."

That proved that Young Otto must have been a hell of a puncher when he fought, because everybody knows that a guy who could punch and couldn't box well always favored a boxer for some reason. It's something he always wanted to do well and didn't.

Anyway, that was a great night at Eastern Parkway. Every seat was taken and it was an exciting fight, and when I went to the box office after the show I was very happy. We had paid Maxim $10,000, Patterson $5,000, and had used some of the $8,000 TV money to pay the preliminary fighters.

In the box-office I said to Lence, "Well, we made some money tonight." He put his head down without looking at me. I knew something was wrong. I said, "What the hell's the matter?"

Lence said, "Well, Maxim got $10,000, but Doc Kearns got hold of me during the week and said he needed $1,500 for walking-around money. He said he needed to take care of certain people to see that we got publicity. He said you had put your O.K. on it."

"Me? I never okayed anything," I screamed. "You sucker. He took you for fifteen hundred that could have been your profit."

That was Kearns for you. He had managed Jack Dempsey and Mickey Walker, and had lived on his wits all his life. I couldn't scream, because Kearns had let me have Maxim's service even though he was tied in with Jim Norris. I was grateful to managers who gave me their fighters. Marv Jensen was one of those managers.

Jensen was a guy out of Utah who had never had a fighter box in New York until I brought Gene Fullmer in. Fullmer was Jensen's fighter and while he was well known in the West, he had

47

never fought east of Pittsburgh until I brought him in to Eastern Parkway.

The day Fullmer and Jensen arrived in New York, they checked into a hotel and then went to the CYO Gym on the West Side to work out. I went over to have a look at Fullmer. After all, I had never seen him fight and didn't know what I had bought. All I knew about him was that he was a Mormon. He was scheduled to fight a pretty tough Bronx kid named Jackie LaBua and I was worried.

Fullmer did not spar that first day in New York. What he did was to loosen up on the floor, shadow-boxing and just moving around. I took one look at him and turned green. He had two left feet, no left hand, no right hand. If I ever saw an uncoordinated athlete, that was Gene Fullmer. It seemed to me that Fullmer could not even spell fight. I started to sweat.

"Hey, Marv," I said to Jensen. "How much did your transportation from Utah cost?"

"Plane fare was $600," the manager said.

"Could you come to my office, please? I'll give you back the $600 and add a few dollars. Take this kid back to Utah. He can't fight at all. He's going to disgrace us."

The manager looked at me and smiled. He was a light-skinned guy with blue eyes and blond hair combed straight back. He looked like a real hick, but he was a pretty shrewd guy. In the years ahead I learned to like him a lot, but on that day in the CYO Gym I wished I had never seen him.

"Let me tell you something, Teddy," Jensen said. "Don't worry about this kid. He doesn't look good in the gym, but he's a tough, natural brawler. Go with him."

What was I going to do? I said, "All right. He's here and the fight's coming up in four days. You signed for the fight in good faith, so there's nothing for me to do. I can't make you go home, so we'll go through with the fight.

48

The fight went off and Fullmer got the decision, but the next day an old fight man named Johnny Attell called me and asked, "What happened to your main event last night?"

I said, "What do you mean, Johnny?" He said, "I tuned in late and watched the last part of the fight. I thought the main event ended early and that I was watching an emergency bout."

"Go on," I said. I was getting mad. "That was Fullmer beating LaBua in a pretty good fight."

"Fullmer? Was that Fullmer? And you had to go to Utah to get him? What a waste of money," Attell said.

I got off the phone and kicked my desk, and I thought, What the hell does a guy want, anyway? That was a good, hard fight. I was still angry when my phone rang again. It was bad news. One of the fighters in my main event next week was sick and wouldn't be able to fight. I needed a substitute to fight Peter Muller, a German middleweight.

It was only six days before the show and I had to act fast. It struck me that maybe Fullmer was still in town, though he was supposed to take an early train back to Salt Lake City. So I called his hotel. He and Jensen had checked out and were on their way to the airport. I called the airplane, but the plane for Salt Lake City had taken off. "Can you get Mr. Jensen to call me when he arrives in Salt Lake City?" I asked.

A few hours later Jensen called. "What's up, Teddy?" he asked. I told him about the break in next week's card. Would he come back and fight Peter Muller for me next Monday night?

"Sure, why not," the manager said. "Gene came out of the fight last night unmarked. He's ready."

The following day they got on a plane and came back to New York, and Fullmer gave Muller a pretty good going over in ten rounds the next Monday night.

It wasn't easy keeping Eastern Parkway going. Jim Norris tried everything to knock me out of the box. When I made a

49

match, I was never sure the International Boxing Club would not try to break it up. I wondered why they did not do more to undermine Eastern Parkway. People whispered to me that Lence wasn't really the owner of the fight club. They said that James Plumeri, alias Jimmy Doyle, was Lence's partner. When Thomas E. Dewey was the District Attorney in Manhattan he had sent Doyle to Sing Sing as a garment district racketeer. By the time we were operating Eastern Parkway, Doyle was both an undercover owner of several dress manufacturing companies and a licensed fight manager. Because Lence also was in the garment business, boxing people assumed he was tied up with Doyle.

One day Lence told me, "We got to go have a meet with Doyle. He wants to see you." So we went down to the garment center and stood on the sidewalk drinking egg creams in front of a candy store. Pretty soon, Doyle came along. Like most mob guys, he was nattily dressed and his black hair was plastered to his skull. He said hello and then he said, "Listen, I want you to use a fighter of mine in Eastern Parkway. That's why we're having this meet."

"Who's the fighter?" I asked, and he said, "Gaby Ferland, from Montreal."

"I know him," I said. "He's not bad."

"What date can you give me for him?" Doyle asked.

I looked at my calendar and I said, "About three weeks from next Monday. I'll put him in an eight-round semi-final."

"Semi-final?" Doyle said. He sneered. "Semi-final, my ass. I don't want him in no semi-final. I want him in a main event."

"Look, I'm using better fighters than Gaby Ferland in the main events. Like last Monday we had Robert Villemain and José Basora. I can't use Ferland in a main bout."

"You put Ferland in a main event or you'll never get another fighter in Eastern Parkway. You can close the club tomorrow. You're finished." He almost spit in my face but I stared at him and said, "Well, then there's no use talking. If we're finished, we're finished. I'm not going to put your boy in a main event. If Lence wants him, let him be the matchmaker."

I turned and walked away, and Lence came running after me. He said, "Teddy, if you don't want Gaby Ferland in a main event, he's not going to be in a main event."

Doyle went around trying to get Eastern Parkway boycotted, but he couldn't stop me from going out and getting fighters from all over the country, the way I got Gene Fullmer. Besides, I learned long ago that mob guys will back off if you stand up to them, at least in boxing.

The funny thing about that is that Doyle himself taught me that. Or, at least he had a hand in teaching me a lesson I'll never forget. What happened was that one night I went up to the old Bronx Coliseum to watch Eddie Alzek fight. Irving Cohen was his manager and in those days I went every place Irving went.

This Tuesday night we drove up to the Coliseum, way up in the Bronx, and Alzek is fighting a six-round bout. He got the decision and after the fight, we went to his dressing room to wait for him to get dressed.

At the Bronx Coliseum they had only two dressing rooms. Fighters on one side of the card would dress in one room. Their opponents would dress in the second room. In that way they were kept apart until they actually got into the ring.

One of the fighters in Alzek's dressing room was Doug Marsh, a Canadian who was in the main event. Jimmy Doyle managed Marsh in partnership with a fellow named Sammy Aaronson. I knew Aaronson. He was a skinny guy with a stable of fighters bigger than the Royal Canadian Mounted Police. If you needed a fighter at five o'clock in the afternoon to fight that night, Aaronson could find one for you. Later, when I became a matchmaker, I learned how important it was to have a guy like him around. He saved many a matchmaker from committing suicide.

Marsh was a pretty good fighter, however, and Aaronson paid a lot of attention to him, maybe because Doyle had a piece of him. Well, what happened was that Marsh forgot to bring his foul-proof cup to the Coliseum the night we were there.

"What the hell am I gonna do?" he asked, and Alzek, who was a pretty nice kid, offered to lend him his foul-proof cup, which is worn over the genitals for protection. Marsh accepted the offer.

After the fight, Marsh came running back to the dressing room trailed by Doyle. The decision in the fight had been a draw and Doyle was berating the Canadian for fighting a bad fight. "What the hell was the matter?" Doyle asked, and the fighter said, "Geez, Jimmy, that cup I was wearing was so tight, it was strangling me. I couldn't fight. I couldn't move. I couldn't do nothing."

"Why the hell didn't you tell me?" Doyle said. "I was in the corner with you. We could have done something." Then, grabbing a pair of scissors, Doyle said to Marsh angrily, "Turn around. I'll cut that lousy cup off you."

Hearing this, Alzek laughed at Doyle, grabbed him by the throat and said, "You gonna cut my cup! I'll punch you right in the mouth!" Doyle turned white with fear. He backed off and I grabbed Alzek and cooled him off. Doyle didn't do a thing to show how tough he was. That taught me a good lesson. I never backed off from a tough guy in all my years in boxing. That's why, when Doyle tried to get me to use his fighter in a main event at Eastern Parkway, I went right to him and told him off.

When I finally got out of Eastern Parkway, it was not because of Doyle. Television politics was the reason. ABC-TV was trying to move in on boxing and offered Lence $12,000 a week, instead of the $8,000 he was getting from Dumont, to take over the program at Eastern Parkway. At first, he couldn't make a move because he was tied up with Dumont, but then he dissolved his promotional company.

This allowed him to sign with ABC, and Dumont, eager to stay in boxing, to make a deal on its own with the London Sporting Club, Inc., to teleview their shows from the St. Nicholas Arena in direct competition with the Monday night fights from Eastern Parkway.

That was a bad deal all around. By competing with each other, the networks were dividing their boxing audience. Ratings went down. ABC-TV was very unhappy at Eastern Parkway. At the St. Nick's bad things were happening. The New York State Athletic Commission discovered the London Sporting Club was a "front" for the New York Boxing Guild, a "union" of fight managers. The Guild was outlawed and the St. Nick's license was revoked. Dumont wanted to stay in boxing and some of the executives asked me if I would be interested in promoting at the St. Nicholas Arena.

"How about it?" I asked Lence.

"Take it, Teddy," he said. "We're not going to last much longer here in Brooklyn."

I accepted the proposition from Dumont and formed a corporation to promote fights. My wife, Judy, and I were the only officers of the corporation. In my four years with Dumont I made a lot of money and when I gave up St. Nick's to go to work for Madison Square Garden Boxing, Inc., in 1959, I gave the club to my office manager. That's how I repaid Irving Cohen for getting me into boxing.

The D.A.
Says I'm O.K.

In January 1959, the United States Supreme Court sustained a lower court decision declaring Norris's International Boxing Club a monopoly in the restraint of trade. Norris was ordered to resign from Madison Square Garden, to sell all his Garden stock within five years, and to dissolve the IBC in New York and Illinois. Boxing guys like me were happy.

I knew Norris was a nice guy who just couldn't get along without the company of gangsters like "Golfbag" Sam Hunt, a killer from Chicago who got the name because he carried his guns in a golfbag, and Frankie Carbo, who killed people and owned fighters and made champions at will. That was the sad thing about Norris. He had millions and could have done a lot of good for boxing. Instead, he went the wrong way and got caught.

After the Supreme Court acted, Norris decided that he did not want to wait five years to get out of the Garden. With his partner, Arthur Wirtz, he put his stock up for sale, and within a month or so it was bought for about $4 million by the Graham-

Paige Corporation. The new owners came in, organized Madison Square Garden Boxing, Inc., and named Harry Markson the director of boxing. Markson called me one day and asked me to have lunch with him. I knew what was in the wind. He wanted me to become the matchmaker at Madison Square Garden. It took me thirty seconds to accept.

"You'll have a free hand," Markson promised. "There are no more tough guys, there are no favors, there are no more obligations. You have nobody to answer but me. Ned Irish is still in the Garden and he will be my boss and I will be your boss, and we'll get along."

Irish was a good man. I always thought of him as the best executive in the whole history of Madison Square Garden. That's saying a lot because the Garden is more than 100 years old. It would be fun working with him. But immediately there was a minor problem. When Markson told Admiral Bergen that he had hired me, the chairman of the board wondered why he had done this without clearing it.

"I knew you wanted Brenner," the Admiral said, "but I didn't know you were offering him the job."

"Sorry, Admiral," Markson said, "but I wanted to ask Brenner first to make sure we could get him."

The Admiral went into action. He asked Irish to call his friend, Frank Hogan, the district attorney of New York County, to check on me. The reason was simple. At the time, Hogan was in the middle of an investigation of boxing. A lot of people got indicted, including Frankie Carbo, who pleaded guilty to acting as an undercover manager and got two years on Riker's Island.

When Irish called Hogan, the district attorney said, "We've got nothing on Brenner. Nothing at all." Irish brought the news to the Admiral, who immediately called Markson. "Brenner's O.K.," the Admiral said.

I was walking on air. I was going back to the Garden for my third term there, but this time I was going in not as the assistant matchmaker but as the matchmaker. If I screwed up I would have only myself to blame. It took me twenty years to blow my job.

I couldn't have come back to the Garden at a worse time. We were still running the Gillette fights on Friday nights and there was a scarcity of good fighters. Floyd Patterson was the world heavyweight champion but he would not fight for us because Cus D'Amato had a beef with the Garden. That was funny. I started Patterson off at Eastern Parkway, yet I couldn't get him to fight for the Garden because D'Amato said gangsters ran the boxing in the building. He wasn't the only problem.

Under the federal court decree that knocked Norris out of the box, the Garden was not allowed to sign fighters to exclusive contracts or to return bouts. And for five years the Garden could not put on more than two world championship bouts in any calendar year. I beat the rap for a long time.

I got lucky almost immediately. The fights I put into the Garden were wars. And I was able to make matches because I knew the managers of almost every available fighter in the country. If I didn't know the manager of a certain fighter I always knew somebody who knew him. I made matches nobody believed could be made. I worked twenty-four hours a day to keep the Garden going and I succeeded.

We made deals with promoters in other towns like Miami Beach and Cleveland and Syracuse to put fights in their arenas when the Garden was occupied, and in that way we kept our contract with Gillette going.

In Syracuse, Norman Rothschild was the local promoter. He had been around when Norris and the tough guys were running boxing and he knew the ropes. He was a good guy who worked hard at whatever he did—a dead-honest guy who had a nice family and tried to do the right thing in all things. I liked him and I liked doing business with him.

About a year or so after I became the Garden matchmaker, I put a show in Syracuse on a Friday night. Rothschild was the promoter, of course, but the way we worked it, we would give him a piece of our television receipts to put on a show and he would keep all the gate receipts. That was a big help to smaller promoters, but it also was a help to us, because Madison Square Garden had hockey and basketball and the circus to accommodate. When these events were in the building, we went elsewhere with the boxing, which was sponsored by Gillette on a fifty-two-week basis.

The match I made in Syracuse was between Charlie Powell and Mike DeJohn. They were big heavyweights who were capable of knocking you out with one punch. The trouble was that they had a tendency to lay back and wait. This kind of matchmaking is not the best, but I knew that if I could get Powell and DeJohn excited I would get a good fight out of them.

Besides, Powell had played in the National Football League and was an attraction. So was Mike DeJohn, who was born and grew up in Syracuse and came from a family of fighting brothers. He was a local hero. Powell was managed by a fellow from Los Angeles named Suey Welch. The manager was well-known in Hollywood, where he once handled the career of Mae West.

Before Powell and DeJohn went into the ring, I kept thinking, What can I do to make this a fight? I walked around the arena worrying, and then it came to me. I went to Powell's dressing room and said hello to the heavyweight. Then, hanging my head, I said, "Geez, that DeJohn shouldn't talk that way." "What way?" Powell asked. "He called you a yellow bastard," I said. "He's going to knock your head off when the bell rings, flatten you with one punch." Powell fell for the gag. "I'll throw the first punch," he said.

Then I went to DeJohn's dressing room and pulled the same thing. "What's the matter with that Charlie Powell, Mike?" I said to the fighter. He asked, "What's the matter? What happened?" "He says no Italian's got guts," I told DeJohn. "He says he's going to knock you out with one punch."

You should have seen DeJohn. "That son of a bitch said that about me?" DeJohn said. "Wait till the fight starts."

When I left his room I almost died laughing. I stopped in the men's room on my way to my ringside seat.

Now the fight started and both Powell and DeJohn came charging out of their corners. They both threw right-hand punches. DeJohn nailed Powell, who went down. He got up at the count of nine and was knocked down again, again for the count of nine. When he got up, DeJohn hit him so hard I thought he would go through the ring floor. The referee stopped the fight. It had lasted only forty-seven seconds. That was a record for Gillette fights, but people were happy with the fight because it was exciting and the hometown kid won it.

That broke my own record for a fast knockout, at least in a match made by me. In 1948, when I was in the Garden for the first time, I made a match between Joe Baksi and Gino Buonvino for the St. Nicholas Arena. Baksi was a big, lumbering, strong heavyweight from the Pennsylvania coal mines, and Buonvino was a tough kid from Italy. It was a good match because Baksi had just come back from England, where he had knocked out Freddie Mills in six rounds. Buonvino was strong and could take a punch, and I thought he could make a good fight against Baksi.

The bout was set for Friday night on the Gillette Cavalcade of Sports radio broadcast, but on Wednesday I got word that Baksi wasn't going to fight. His manager was Nate Wolfson, a skinny guy with a sad face who always seemed on the verge of breaking into tears. When Wolfson came to tell me that Baksi was pulling out of the fight because he had hurt his right hand in the gymnasium, I couldn't even look at him. He was so sad, I thought I'd start crying. He did.

Now I was stuck for a fight. The way boxing is these days, it is almost impossible to fill a main event in two days. In

1948 there were plenty of heavyweights available. The only trouble was that all of them seemed to be training for fights their managers had booked.

Even Lee Savold was booked for a bout the next night in Fall River, Mass. Savold was managed by Bill Daly, and Daly was so shrewd, other fight managers had to get up very early in the morning to beat him at his game, which was to hustle a buck wherever a buck was available. He is still around today, eighty-two years of age and going strong, still on the prowl, still hustling a buck.

The reason I said "even Lee Savold" was that Savold was in kind of a doghouse around New York. A few months before he had been knocked out at Ebbets Field by Elmer (Violent) Ray. The end came in two rounds and when the fight was over, fight guys laughed and said the ring was very wet even though not a drop of rain had fallen.

I got in touch with Daly and told him about the break in the card. I said, "Bill, would Savold be available?" Daly said, "Well, Teddy, he's in very good shape because he's been training for the fight in Fall River, but what are we going to do about Sam Silverman? If we take Savold away his promotion in Fall River ain't worth a damn."

"Tell you what, Bill," I said, "we'll compensate him. If Silverman gets a substitute for Savold and runs tomorrow night, we'll pay him his losses, with a little extra on the side. If he can't get a sub, we'll pay him, too, and in that way he'll have no loss, maybe a little profit."

"I'll talk to him," Daly said.

Half an hour later, Daly was back on the phone. "I called Silverman," he said. "Everything's O.K."

I went to see Eddie Eagan. Tom Dewey had named him chairman of the New York State Athletic Commission. Eagan had been a great amateur boxer, the light-heavyweight gold-medal winner at the 1920 Olympic Games. He also made Olympic history in the 1932 Winter Games as a member of the United States four-man bobsled team that won at Lake Placid. He had also been a Rhodes Scholar out of Yale and when Dewey named him chairman of the boxing board, everybody expected great things from him. He came in with a blaze of glory, but went out quietly in 1951 in the midst of one of boxing's numerous investigations. But in 1948, when I went to see him to get approval to substitute Savold against Buonvino, he was strongly entrenched as chairman.

"Under no circumstances will I allow Savold to fight a main event in the Garden," Eagan told me. "He's not qualified. His behavior doesn't call for it."

I said, "Commissioner, whatever you say is true, but this I can tell you, Savold is in condition for this fight because I have been watching him in the gym. He took off twenty pounds for a fight in Massachusetts. I've checked with other people in whom I have confidence. They tell me he's in shape. Besides, Buonvino is not a puncher and I think it'll be a good fight."

"I won't approve it," Eagan said.

That's when it was time to make a grandstand play. I reached into a pocket and pulled out my matchmaker's license. I threw it on Eagan's desk and said, "Commissioner, I'll bet my license on the fight. If Savold doesn't give a good performance, you can take my license and tear it up."

I had him. He couldn't back away from a sporting proposition. He said, "Teddy, we're very happy with the job you've been doing as Chickie Bogard's assistant in the Garden. I'd hate to call your bluff."

"No bluff, Commissioner," I said. "You can pick up my matchmaker's license if Savold makes a bad fight."

Eagan got up from his desk and paced the floor. He stopped, looked me in the eyes and said, "All right. If you feel

61

that strongly about it, I'll approve Savold for the Garden."

That Friday night, Savold came bouncing into the Garden ring, feinted, and then hit Buonvino on the chin with a great left hook. The Italian heavyweight went down and took the count. The fight lasted fifty-seven seconds. Buonvino shit in his pants. I mean that. They had a terrible time cleaning up the ring.

Las Vegas, Here We Come!

For a while, after I went into the Garden, we were competing with Jim Norris. He was running fights on Wednesday nights in the Chicago Stadium, which he owned, and we were running in the Garden on Friday nights. Both shows were on home TV. We were competing for talent, and there was not much talent around.

Television had knocked most neighborhood clubs out of business. People just were not willing to pay to watch two ordinary fighters in the flesh when they could turn on their own TV sets for free to see first-class fighters in action.

About this time some good things happened. Emile Griffith came along. And I discovered Las Vegas.

I got a call one day from Ash Resnick. He was a guy I knew from school in Brooklyn. Now he was a big casino man in Las Vegas. He was in the Thunderbird Hotel, where he was running the casino. When he called me all he wanted to talk about was boxing. "Teddy," he said, "why don't you come out here and run some shows for TV? We got a great building, the Convention Center, seats about nine thousand, and a couple of good guys in the Silver State Boxing Club are running small fights out here."

"I know Silver State," I said. "That's Mel Greb's thing, ain't it?"

"Yeah, he's in with Jack Doyle," Resnick said.

"I remember Greb when he was a kid around Newark when I was promoting there," I said. "Let me think about it, Ash. I'll get back to you."

I talked to Markson about it. In all the years I was associated with Markson, he never was tough on me. We'd disagree and we'd argue, but if I could convince him I was right about something, he'd go along. The idea of Las Vegas appealed to him.

"Let's go out and talk to the people," he said. So I called Ash Resnick back and told him we were coming to Las Vegas and he set up a meet with Greb and Doyle. When Greb and Doyle met us they had Jim Deskin with them. He was the secretary of the Nevada Boxing Commission. We worked out a deal to televise fights out of the Las Vegas Convention Center.

The way it worked, Greb and Doyle, as the Silver State Boxing Club, actually promoted the fights. What we did was to guarantee the promotion so much out of the TV money. And the promotion got most of the gate receipts. We paid the fighters' purses, of course. It was a good deal for Silver State.

At the time, Don Jordan was the world welterweight champion. He was splitting up with Don Nesseth, who, with Jackie Leonard, his partner in the management of Jordan, had been the target of the extortion conspiracy for which Carbo and Palermo went to prison. Jordan told Nesseth, "I'm getting $85,000 for fighting Benny Paret. You take the whole purse and then we're through. After this fight, I got Kirk Kerkorian for my manager."

Kerkorian was a former fighter who was a financial wizard and wound up owning 47 percent of the common stock of the MGM film company.

On May 27, 1960, big-time boxing came to Las Vegas. Jordan and Paret fought for the welterweight title in the Convention Center. After fifteen rounds, Paret got the decision. Kerkorian came to me and said, "Teddy, I understand there's a return-bout contract with Paret, isn't there?"

"Not that I know," I said.

"There is one and you know it," said Kerkorian, who was interested in a title bout for his boy. "Truman Gibson gave it to Nesseth."

"Then let him put it on," I said. I was being a smartass. By then, Gibson, Carbo, Palermo, and their confederates had been indicted by a federal grand jury in Los Angeles. Norris was out of the boxing business. The contract for a return bout between Jordan and Paret wasn't worth the paper it was written on.

I said to Kerkorian, "Look, Kirk, Madison Square Garden can't sign return-bout contracts. That's because of the antitrust decision. We can't get involved in anything like that."

"You promised," he said. "And I got the contract."

"What's the sense of talking," I said. Kerkorian, who was a real smart man with a lot of drive, almost blew his top. I liked him and I wanted to do something for him. I said, "Kirk, listen to me. I'll put you in with Basilio. If you lick him, I guarantee I'll get Jordan another title fight with Paret."

Kerkorian wouldn't stand still for the proposal. "I'm going to court," he said. "I'll see you in court." But after a few weeks, he cooled off. I got Jordan a match with Basilio in Syracuse ten months later. Basilio was all washed up, but he still had enough left to beat Jordan. One fight later, Basilio retired. Jordan lasted another year. He never fought Paret again and he never won another fight.

At the time Paret took the title from Jordan, I knew Emile Griffith would soon be prominent enough to challenge him for the 147-pound title. I liked Griffith from the first day Gil Clancy brought him around to my office in the Garden.

The fighter worked in Howie Albert's millinery factory before he went into the ring and it was Albert who started him in boxing. Griffith was a kid out of St. Thomas in the Virgin Islands who had no more thought of becoming a fighter than he dreamed of owning Madison Square Garden. He was twenty years of age when Albert put him into the Golden Gloves in New York. Griffith surprised everybody by taking a title.

"I got a hell of a kid," Clancy told me. "Emile Griffith."

"Boy or girl?" I asked.

"Stop kidding, Teddy," Clancy said. "He's a hell of a kid and a good fighter."

Clancy brought him around. Griffith laughed a lot and seemed easy to handle. I had known about him in the Golden Gloves and when Clancy turned him pro and I used him in the Garden, I could see he was going to be a hell of a fighter. I used him so often, people started to say I cut in on his earnings.

When I was making matches in the Garden, I never let anything stand in my way. Even if I disliked a certain fighter's manager and I wanted to use the fighter, I swallowed my pride and went after him. When Clancy came around with Griffith, I didn't care one way or another about him. I first knew Clancy when he was a teacher in a junior high school in Brooklyn. He taught physical education and had a few amateur boxers under his wing. I could take him or leave him.

Before I got to the Garden in 1959, Clancy couldn't get himself arrested in the place. He would ask for a manager's ticket for a fight and the matchmaker, whether he was Al Weill or Billy Brown, would say, "Get the hell out of here. Who made you a manager?" He was a nobody. Griffith changed everything for him.

Maybe I'm saying all this badly. What I really believe is that a manager can make or break a fighter. No good manager ever accepts a match he thinks will not benefit his fighter. Either he takes it to advance the fighter's career or for the money he and the fighter can make.

A matchmaker looks at it in another way. He should make only fights that benefit his club. It's up to the manager to protect the fighter. Irving Cohen had a theory. He used to say that when a matchmaker offered him a match for one of his fighters, he would say, "Let's not talk about money. First, let's find out who you want my boy to fight. If I like the opponent, the money will be secondary." That's why his fighters lasted a long time.

Clancy was that kind of manager. Griffith fought for nineteen years and won the welterweight and middleweight title five times. He had a dozen title fights in Madison Square Garden, all during the time I was the matchmaker. Whenever I needed a big fight, I would always depend on him.

He wasn't a knockout puncher—not a one-punch knockout guy—but he always made a good showing, and usually won the close decisions. That is why people in boxing kept whispering that I had a piece of Griffith's contract. In a close bout you could almost always depend on Emile to get it.

Let me say something about scoring a fight. First of all, there are no schools where a guy can learn how to score. There are no firm rules. It is a matter of opinion. It's like judging figure-skating. I've seen one judge in the Winter Olympics give a skater a 9.6 and another judge give the same skater 8.3, and who the hell can tell the difference? It's a judgment call, strictly an opinion.

The one night there was no difference of opinion in a Garden fight involving Griffith was the night he hit Paret so hard and so often in the Garden ring, Paret died of brain injuries ten days later. People had all kinds of theories about that fight. I think it was an unfortunate accident.

Some said Paret actually had been hurt in a street brawl some months before the fight. Others said that Griffith was intent

67

on maiming him because he had challenged Griffith's manhood during the weigh-in for their fatal fight. Who knows?

The doctors said Paret was in good shape going into the fight. But even that did not prove anything. I say that because I remember the story they tell about one ringside doctor who approved a match for a fighter who had suffered a broken kneecap six months before.

In the course of the fight, the kneecap broke again and the wounded fighter, jumping around like a chicken on one leg, tried to throw punches at the guy he was fighting. They stopped it, of course, and the doctor who had passed the fighter as fit rushed back to a phone to call an ambulance. While waiting for somebody to answer his call, the doctor leaned over the desk he was seated at and told a boxing writer, "I knew the knee would break again. I made a bundle betting on the other guy."

Griffith had eleven title fights in Madison Square Garden and fought for us outdoors at Shea Stadium, but this does not mean that I controlled him or had a piece of him or Clancy.

I remember once I wanted Griffith for a welterweight championship bout in the Garden, but Clancy took him to London instead to defend his title against an Englishman named Brian Curvis. That shows how much control I had of the fighter. Just before this happened, I had another run-in with Clancy, who was supposed to be my partner.

Gillette always liked to run a big show just before Christmas to kick off the sales season for their blades and razors. So they came to Harry Markson and said, "Can we get a title fight around December to get us started on our Christmas campaign?" Markson promised them a title fight and I called Clancy to see if we could get Griffith.

"Can't, Teddy," Clancy said. "Just talked to my accountant and he said Emile's made too much money. A title fight would put us in a higher bracket because we'd make too much money out of it."

"Son of a bitch," I said. "We need you."

"We'll fight a non-title fight for you," Clancy said. "That'll be all right."

Markson went back to Gillette and told the people there we couldn't get a title fight. They were willing to take another fight in its place, so long as a champion was in it. So I made Griffith with Hurricane Carter for Pittsburgh five days before Christmas.

"It's a tough fight," I warned Clancy.

"We'll take it," Clancy said. "It's not a title fight and we'll get some money for Christmas. I'm not worried."

"You ought to be," I told Clancy. "Don't be surprised if Emile loses, even gets knocked out."

"Stop, Teddy," Clancy said. "It's just another fight."

"I'm telling you to get Emile in good shape. He's going to need condition to go ten rounds with Hurricane Carter."

What happened was that Griffith went out to Pittsburgh and was knocked out by Carter in the first round. It was the very first time Griffith was ever knocked out. The fellow who flattened him is now doing hard time in New Jersey prison for murder. He almost killed Griffith in their fight.

Just before Griffith went to Pittsburgh to be knocked out by Carter he was voted the winner of the Edward J. Neil Memorial Award by the Boxing Writers Association. It was a big honor and Griffith was happy. Then he went to Pittsburgh and got flattened, and when he stood up on the dais at the writers' award dinner to accept the Neil Trophy, he said, "Something funny happened to me on my way to the dinner. I stopped off in Pittsburgh." He brought the house down. Everybody roared but me, because I knew Clancy could have avoided the knockout fight by fighting for the title in Madison Square Garden.

By this time we were moving pretty good in the Garden. Gene Fullmer was the National Boxing Association's world middleweight champion and I could always use him because I had given him his first bout in New York when I was at Eastern Parkway. He boxed for us whenever we needed him and finally, in 1961, we booked him for a title fight in Vegas with Sugar Ray Robinson.

Robinson was the greatest all-round fighter I've ever seen. Being a middleweight, he couldn't punch like Joe Louis, naturally, but no fighter I ever knew could move another guy around the way Robinson could before taking him out with combination punches.

By 1961, when I had him fighting Fullmer in Las Vegas, he had been a pro for twenty-one years. A few months before he had boxed a draw with Fullmer in Los Angeles, but now, in Las Vegas, he was determined to win the middleweight title for the sixth time.

Two days before the fight, he showed up at the Convention Center, where they were setting up the ring for the bout. He looked at it and said, "Teddy, how big is that ring?" I said, "I don't know, Ray, but I'll ask Mel Greb." I asked Greb, who said, "It's sixteen feet eight inches from rope to rope." I couldn't believe it. "That small?" I said. "Yeah, what do you expect, a ballroom?" Greb said.

I told Robinson the dimensions and he looked me in the eye and said, "I'm not fighting. Forget it, I'm not fighting. You get a twenty-foot ring or there's no fight."

George Gainford, Robinson's advisor, said, "You're right, Ray. No big ring, no fight."

"Where the hell are we going to get a twenty-foot ring?" I asked.

"That's your business, not ours," Gainford said.

I talked to Greb and suggested that he call Los Angeles. If there was a twenty-foot ring in California, they could truck it into Las Vegas in time for the fight. At least, that's what I thought.

Greb came back after calling California. He whispered,

70

"Hey, Teddy, they got an eighteen-foot ring in L.A. That's the biggest they have." I said, "My god! This one is sixteen feet, eight inches and they have an eighteen-foot ring there, and Ray wants a twenty-foot ring. What the hell are we going to do?"

I bluffed. I went over to Sugar Ray and said, "We're trying to get a ring out of Los Angeles. If you have patience we're trying to contact the people to put a bigger ring on a truck and truck it here for the fight."

"O.K., O.K., long as it's a twenty-foot ring," Robinson said.

When Robinson left the building, I told Greb, "Call L.A. See if we can get that eighteen-foot ring shipped in here."

Again he called L.A. He was told that nothing could be done until the next day. But the next day, when Greb called back, he was told that it was too late, the ring could not be trucked in fast enough to get it to Las Vegas for the fight.

We didn't tell Robinson or Gainford this and when Robinson's advisor came back to the Convention Center the next day we gave him a tape measure and told him everything was all right.

Gainford climbed into the ring and, with the help of one of Robinson's retinue, measured the ring. "It's eighteen feet," he said. "It's all right. Robinson'll fight in an eighteen-foot ring. Everything's going to be all right."

When Gainford left, I slapped Greb on the back. "You're a fucking genius," I said. "A real damn genius."

What Greb had done was to cut sixteen inches out of the middle of a tape measure and then had sewn the two pieces together. In that way, when Gainford measured the inside of the sixteen foot, eight-inch ring, it showed eighteen feet on the tape measure.

No sooner were we out of that dilemma than another problem came up. We were having dinner at the Dunes when a newspaperman came rushing in and told us—Admiral Bergen, Harry Markson and myself—that Robinson had just called off the fight. We lost our appetites.

"Let's go see him," Markson suggested. The three of us went to Robinson's suite. It was tough to get him alone. He always traveled with a retinue of a dozen or so, including his own barber and a valet. I guess later, when Muhammad Ali came on the scene, he copied Robinson's way of doing things.

When he finally got Sugar Ray alone, Admiral Bergen said, "Ray, what's the trouble?"

"I want more money for the fight."

"At this late hour you're trying to rewrite the contract you signed? Is that what you're saying?" Admiral Bergen asked Robinson.

"When I signed the contract to give Gillette the right to televise the fight, I signed for the United States rights only. Now the contract reads 'worldwide rights.' Unless I get $10,000 more I'm not fighting."

Admiral Bergen kept talking to Robinson. It didn't do any good. Sugar Ray kept saying, "I did not sign for international television rights. I just signed for the United States rights, and if you want my picture to be shown all over the world you're going to have to pay $10,000 more."

"We'll see about it," Markson said. "Gentlemen, we can always settle this thing one way or the other tomorrow."

The next day, a couple of hours before the fight was to start, Robinson came to the Convention Center and went to his dressing room. There was no agreement yet. He undressed, got into his boxing gear, had his hands wrapped, and still we hadn't settled. He was testing us, knowing we needed the fight to satisfy Gillette.

The fighters were scheduled to get into the ring just before ten o'clock. At five minutes to ten, Markson finally said, "All right, Ray, we'll give you the extra $10,000. Now give us a good fight."

He did, too, though he was forty-one years of age and long past his prime. The fight with Fullmer was so close, it could have gone either way. But Fullmer got the decision and kept the title. Even though Robinson gave us many heartaches, he always gave us a good show. And in boxing that is not always the case.

Robinson had a sense of pride that not only made him a great fighter but also made him a true professional. He not only believed in himself, but he had great respect for other fighters, providing they were good at their trade and believed in themselves and in boxing.

I remember something that happened with him two years after Fullmer beat him in Las Vegas. By then Robinson had been boxing for twenty-three years and was forty-three years of age. Herman Taylor, a promoter in Philadelphia, got hold of me and said, "Teddy, you're friendly with Robinson. He listens to you. I'd like to put him in a fight with Joey Giardello."

"I'll certainly talk to him, Herman," I said. "I'll go up to his apartment in Harlem and see if he'll take the match."

When I told Robinson of Taylor's idea, he said, "Teddy, I don't want the Giardello fight."

"Why not?

"Well, you know I've been boxing professionally now for twenty-three years and that's an awful tough fight with Giardello at this stage. I would have to go into real training and get myself up for the fight. I don't want to do that, even if I can do it. I'd rather say no to Herman, much as I like him. After all, he gave me a lot of fights when I was just starting out in the pros."

It was my turn to speak. I said, "Ray, under ordinary circumstances I'd agree with you. If anybody said to me at this stage that you should fight Giardello, I would say it's a tough fight and you really had to get into good shape to keep from getting hurt. But this case is different."

"What's different?" Sugar Ray asked.

"Well, forgetting Herman Taylor, who you like. I think you should do it for Giardello."

"I owe him nothing," Robinson said.

"Just hold on a minute," I said. "Let me explain something to you." I asked him if he had a copy of *The Ring Record Book* in the apartment. He did. When he got it, I opened to Giardello's record. "Look at this record," I said. "Joey Giardello is one fighter—there aren't many—who never ducked a tough fight with a guy just because the other guy was black."

"I never ducked a white guy," Robinson said, and we laughed.

"Look at these black fighters Giardello fought. Gil Turner, Johnny Saxton, Willie Troy, Tiger Jones, Rory Calhoun, Randy Sandy, Jesse Smith, Holly Mims, Henry Hank, Hurricane Carter, George Benton. He never skipped anybody, and the only great black fighter not on his record is Sugar Ray Robinson. He's also winding down his career, like you, and he has a chance for a payday and you're saying no to him. He deserves a shot."

Robinson said, "You know, Teddy, I hadn't realized that Giardello boxed all those tough guys. Call Herman. Tell him it's all right. I'll box Giardello."

Robinson just couldn't get himself up for the fight. He needed more time to train because he was old and old guys have to work harder than young guys to get into shape. One thing about Robinson, he would never get into the ring unless he at least looked trim. He had too much pride to look like a fat old man. He tried hard to beat Giardello, but at the end of ten rounds, Giardello got the decision. If the fight had taken place a few years earlier, Sugar Ray would have won.

To this day, Giardello says that it was Robinson who made it possible for him to win the world middleweight title. The victory over Sugar Ray moved Giardello up as a contender and he won the championship from Dick Tiger in his very next fight.

Robinson continued to box for two years after he was

beaten by Giardello. His last fight was with Joey Archer in Pittsburgh on November 10, 1965, just twenty-five years after his first
bout, a four-rounder in Madison Square Garden on October 4,
1940. He had spanned a lot of history, from the first days of
World War II to the war in Vietnam.

The promoter of Sugar Ray's last fight was a young
hustler named Don Elbaum who had a sense of drama and a
touch of the poet. He could make more touches in shorter time
than anybody else in the boxing business.

In Pittsburgh, a couple of days before Robinson's fare-
well fight with Archer, Elbaum threw a party for the old great
fighter. Robinson showed up with Millie Bruce, whom he had re-
cently married. At the party, Elbaum presented a package to
Robinson. He was serious and said to Sugar Ray, "I've kept the
things in this package for twenty-five years and I thought it ap-
propriate to give them to you tonight."

"Thanks," Robinson said. "What's in the package?"

"I'll open it and show you," the promoter said, and he
did. "These gloves," he said to Robinson, "are the very boxing
gloves you wore in your very first fight in Madison Square
Garden twenty-five years ago. Don't ask me how I got hold of
them, but here they are."

Sugar Ray looked at the gloves and his eyes filled. He
looked at his wife, Millie, and there were tears in her eyes, too.
He tried to speak, but he was all choked up. Al Abrams, a sports
editor in Pittsburgh, broke the ice.

"Hey, Ray, put on the old gloves so we can get a picture
for the paper," Abrams said loudly.

Elbaum was frantic. "No, Ray, no picture with the gloves
on," the promoter screamed. "Just hold the gloves together to
show them. That'll make a picture."

Robinson didn't hear and tried to get the gloves on. He

couldn't. They were both right-handed gloves. "You son of a bitch," he said to Elbaum, who ran away. Two nights later, Robinson lost his last fight. He didn't bother to take his gloves home as souvenirs.

The Ten-Dollar Champion

When I say Sugar Ray Robinson was the greatest fighter I ever saw, it's not horseshit. I mean it, but I don't mean that I do not appreciate other great fighters. When a guy has been around as long as I have, he can't remember all the fighters he has watched. It is enough if he remembers boxers like Ike Williams. He was the best lightweight I've ever seen.

Williams came out of New Jersey and won the lightweight title in 1947 and lost it in 1951, when he was all through and ready to hang them up. He was managed by Blinky Palermo and that should tell you a lot, except that Blinky could never make him do any jobs. He was proud to be a fighter.

He could do everything. He hit hard and was a smart boxer, and he could take a punch. And he had his head on straight. One day, when he was all through, I said to him, "Ike, I'd like to have a pup out of you." He said, "Why me? You want a pup, get Sugar Ray Robinson's pup."

"You were a great fighter, Ike," I said.

"Hell, no," Williams said. "The only great fighter I ever

77

saw was a black mother by the name of Sugar Ray Robinson. I was a good fighter He was a great fighter."

Why I bring this up here is that I was fortunate as a matchmaker to be involved early with the guy who called himself "The Greatest." I gave Muhammad Ali his first fight on TV, only then he was known as Cassius Clay and was just a kid out of Louisville, a fast-talking boxer they called the "Louisville Lip."

I knew about him even before he went to Rome to win the gold medal in the 178-pound division in the 1960 Olympic Games. Some of the reporters who had seen him box told me about him, and when he came home from Rome he was taken over by the Louisville Sponsoring Group, which was a bunch of rich white guys in Kentucky and New York who could invest money and thought they could get their jollies by owning a heavyweight champion.

The first time I saw Ali was in Madison Square Garden. He came to my office on his way to the Rome Olympics. What I remember is that he was a good-looking kid with a big mouth. "You're lookin' at the next heavyweight champion of the world," he said. "Can you lend me ten dollars?"

"Lend you ten dollars?" I asked. "What the hell for?"

"For having a good time in Harlem," he said.

I gave him the sawbuck, which he did not forget about the next time I saw him. By this time he had won an Olympic gold medal in Rome and he was on his way back to Louisville. He said, "Remember me?"

"Of course," I said. "You're the next heavyweight champion of the world. Where's my ten dollars?"

"Alway pay my debts," he said, handing me the money. In the next twenty years I never heard of Ali ever stiffing anybody. I got to say that for him.

When he turned pro, the Louisville Sponsoring Group put him in fights in Louisville and Miami Beach. The reporters wrote nice things about him because he scored five knockouts in his first seven bouts.

Angelo Dundee was training him and doing a real fine job, which didn't surprise me. I had known Dundee for years. He was the brother of Chris Dundee, the promoter in Miami Beach, and when Angelo first came around after World War II, he was what we used to call a "towel boy." He worked in corners with fighters trained by other guys and caught on to the business fast. By 1960, when he took over Ali, he was one of the best trainers in the business.

It was good having Dundee with Ali, because he made it easy to do business with the Louisville Sponsoring Group. The members of the Group did not know much about boxing. They took a lot of advice from Angelo. I found that out when I offered Ali his first fight on television. Dundee said. "That's a good match. We'll make it."

The opponent was Alonzo Johnson, who was twenty-seven years old and had had almost thirty bouts and was experienced. He was just the right opponent for the young Louisville heavyweight. In a situation like that, a matchmaker shouldn't look for a soft touch. What he should get is a guy who will test a young fighter in the process of losing.

In this case I wanted a good fight. The fight was scheduled for Louisville, but it was going to be televised by NBC on the Gillette Cavalcade of Sports. The fact that he was going on national TV brought out the ham in Ali. He strutted in front of his neighbors. He boasted to reporters that nobody could keep him from winning the heavyweight championship. Bill King, the Louisville promoter, gave a cocktail party in his honor and Ali promised to kick Johnson's ass. That was exactly what happened. It was a tough fight, but Ali won it. The TV sponsor was happy with the show.

Six weeks later I put Ali into Louisville again, again on

network TV. This time I matched him with a tough Argentinean named Alex Miteff. I thought, Hey, this guy can take a hell of a punch. I want to see if the kid really can hit.

On the day of the bout, Bill King came to the weigh-in with bad news. He had forgotten to order a set of new gloves for the fight. I rushed around Louisville trying to find gloves. Nobody in Kentucky had a new set. They had good racehorses and good Bourbon whisky, but no new boxing gloves that would fit heavyweights. "We're in a hell of a fix," I told King. He said, "Maybe you can get a set shipped in from New York."

I rushed to the phone and called Everlast, the glove manufacturers, and arranged to have a set sent down by plane. "We'll put it on a plane that gets to Louisville by eight-thirty tonight," a salesman at Everlast said. "O.K.," I said. "The main event doesn't start until ten o'clock."

In the meantime, while we were waiting for the gloves to arrive from New York, somebody found a set of old gloves in the local gymnasium. They hadn't been used for a long time and, because they hadn't dried properly, they were hard as rocks.

I asked Gil Clancy, who was Miteff's manager, "Will you let Miteff use them if the other gloves don't get here from New York?"

"Why not?" Clancy said. "I know these gloves are like rocks, but my guy punches harder than the other guy. They'll favor Miteff, if we have to use them."

We waited for the other gloves to arrive on the plane, but when ten o'clock came and they hadn't been delivered, we put the old gloves on the fighters.

It was a close fight for five rounds. The three officials were split on their cards. Miteff was scoring points by going for his opponent's mid-section, while Ali kept sticking and moving, and trying to tie up Miteff in close.

Right at the start of the sixth round, Miteff moved in on

Ali, who let go an uppercut that caught the point of Miteff's chin. The glove on Ali's right fist was so hard, it had twice the effect of an ordinary punch. Miteff went down on his face, out cold, and was counted out. It took twenty minutes for his head to clear. "Can't believe it," Miteff kept saying. "Can't believe it. That guy's no puncher."

I have always believed that Ali was a real good fighter. Others call him great. He believes that he was "The Greatest." What worked real well for him was not his punch or his speed, but his chin. He could take a punch about as good as any heavyweight in the world. Even when Larry Holmes, the World Boxing Council champion, stopped Ali in Las Vegas in 1980, he did not floor him once, bad as Ali was. In his whole career, Ali was down just three times. One of the knockdowns—the first in his pro career—came in his first fight in Madison Square Garden.

Sonny Banks was Ali's opponent in that fight. I picked Banks because I thought he would give Ali a fight without ending the Louisville heavyweight's winning streak. So I made the match and Ali came into New York and Harry Markson threw a luncheon for him. He had been spouting poetry—I guess it was poetry—and picking the round in which he would knock a guy out, and there was great excitement around the Garden.

The luncheon for Ali was at a restaurant down in Greenwich Village where bearded poets came to read their poetry out loud. We thought Ali could get away with a poetry reading. Instead, he stood up and said. "You people got to watch out. Sonny Liston is the heavyweight champion and he's a black man. I'm a black man. You better start developing some white hopes, because I'm going to win the title and I'm going to hold the title so long, they'll forget there ever was a white champion."

I laughed, but I thought, What a fresh punk. He's got a long way to go. Beat Liston? Never!

Sonny Banks was a tough opponent for Ali, or so I

thought, especially when Banks hit him with a left hook to the belly in the fourth round. Ali went down, but to his credit he got up and flattened Banks. I said to myself, Hey, wait a minute. It takes a hell of a fighter to get up and knock the other guy out. Maybe this kid can knock Liston out, not now but later.

More than a year passed before Ali was back in the Garden. By this time he had been around the circuit, knocking out a bunch of old guys, including Archie Moore, and it was about time to put him in with some real competition. So I proposed that he fight a fellow by the name of Doug Jones and Ali's people accepted the match.

Jones was a New York heavyweight who had fought for the world light-heavyweight title and had just missed winning it from Harold Johnson. He boxed well and could punch. In the two fights he had just before the one with Ali, he had knocked out Bob Foster and Zora Folley, and they were good fighters.

We did a smart thing with the fight. Instead of putting it on home TV, we decided to put it on closed-circuit TV. The deal brought Madison Square Garden a hell of a profit, because the company that handled the closed-circuit was run by Lester Malitz and his son, Michael. They did a wonderful job selling the show to exhibitors and the public.

Well, that's not exactly right. Ali sold the show. All the newspapers were on strike. It was the longest newspaper strike in the history of the city and boxing people said the show would be a flop because there were no sports pages around. But Ali went on TV and radio and talked up the fight, and soon after we put the tickets on sale at prices from $2.00 to $12.00, Madison Square Garden was sold out. Nothing like that had happened in years. They were hanging from the rafters.

It's funny what I remember. The day after the fight, Ali met Ned Irish, the president of Madison Square Garden. He said to Irish, "Pretty good crowd we had last night. Well, we finally got the pigeons out of the balcony. They've been there a long time and it took me to get them out."

The fight, however, was no laughing matter. It was so close, people argued about the decision for weeks. The way I saw it, Ali won the fight by rallying in the last two rounds. He proved right then and there that he had stamina and was capable of reaching back to help himself when he needed it. He became a sensation.

Two days after the fight, I got a call from Ed Sullivan. "Can I get the kid for my show?" Sullivan asked. "All I want him to do is to take a bow." I said, "Sure, I'll talk to him." So I talked to the fighter. I said, "Hey, Ed Sullivan wants you to take a bow on his *Toast of the Town* show on TV Sunday." Ali's eyes lit up. "That's for me," he said. "Tell the man I'll be there."

I got in touch with Arthur Grafton in Louisville. He was a very prominent lawyer in Kentucky who was a member of the Louisville Sponsoring Group. I told him about Sullivan's invitation to the fighter. "Maybe you'd better talk to Archie Foster in New York," Grafton said.

I knew Foster. He was in with the Louisville group. I also knew he was a big shot at the Ted Bates Agency, in advertising. So I called him and he said he could see nothing wrong with the fighter going on the Sullivan show so long as he took a bow and did nothing else. "If he does more than that, he'll have to get paid," Foster said. I assured him that all Sullivan wanted was for Ali to take a bow.

Maurice Chevalier was on the *Toast of the Town* that Sunday, and when Ali showed up, Chevalier almost wet his pants. He was a hot fight fan. I heard people say that when he was younger he had sparred with Georges Carpentier, the French fighter who was knocked out by Jack Dempsey. Chevalier and Ali had a long chat about boxing and then the fighter took a seat among the studio audience.

83

Just as Chevalier came on the stage to perform in front of the CBS cameras, Sullivan announced, "Ladies and gentlemen, seated out there in the studio audience is a young man who just beat Doug Jones in a sensational fight in Madison Square Garden. From Louisville, Kentucky, the great Cassius Clay."

Ali immediately got up, took a bow, and trotted up on the stage. He was wearing some sort of a cape and was carrying a cane. Before anyone knew what was happening, he was performing a few childish tricks of magic. Then he thanked Sullivan, thanked Chevalier, and returned to his seat.

The next day I got a call from Archie Foster, who bawled the hell out of me. He said I knew his fighter was going to perform on the Sullivan show and not just take a bow. "That was a dirty trick," he said. I laughed. If it was a trick, only the fighter knew about it, nobody else, not even Sullivan, certainly not me. I told Foster if he didn't forget about the whole thing, I would send a guy over to make him disappear. "What guy?" he said. "Cassius Clay, the magician," I said. He laughed. We both laughed.

Three months later, I went to London to see Ali fight Henry Cooper at Wembley Stadium. Cooper owned a fruit and vegetable market—they called him a greengrocer over there—and was a pretty good fighter, except that he cut easy and bled like a slaughtered cow.

The weigh-in took place at the Palladium, the vaudeville house in which many great American singers and comedians had performed. When the weigh-in was over, Ali went back to his dressing room to pull on his street clothes. In his dressing room hanging over a chair, he found a long purple robe and a gilded papier-mâché crown. Without telling anybody, he took the purple robe and the crown and stuffed it into the bag in which he carried his boxing trunks and shoes.

It rained at Wembley that night. I found myself seated in a front-row seat next to Elizabeth Taylor and Richard Burton.

They almost died laughing when Ali came sauntering down toward the ring all decked out in the purple robe and the gilded papier-mâché crown, acting like he was a king to the music blaring out of the loudspeaker system.

I think Ali's sense of humor offended the English fans, who began booing him while he pranced around the ring with the crown on his head and the purple robe still draped over his shoulders. They take their royalty seriously over there.

I wasn't worried about the fight. Ali could handle Cooper. It didn't take him long to draw blood. What a slicing job he did on Cooper. Right before the end of the fourth round, however, Ali let himself get into trouble. Spotting Elizabeth Taylor and Richard Burton in the front row, he took his mind off the fight long enough to take a peek at the movie stars. Cooper hit him with a left hook flush on the chin. Down went Ali. The referee started to count . . . one . . . two . . . three . four . . . five . . . six. When the count reached six, the bell rang. Ali was saved by the bell.

Angelo Dundee came charging into the ring, followed by the others in Ali's corner. They dragged the American back to his corner and began working on him. What happened next was hard to believe. One of Ali's gloves was split. He needed a new glove to replace it. Fight guys later said that Dundee had pulled the oldest gimmick of all. In between rounds, he had used a razor to slash one glove so that his man could get more than a minute's rest.

Whether he did, I don't know. Until this day Dundee denies it, but by the time a new glove was obtained and laced on Ali's fist, the fighter had an extra rest of maybe four minutes. He was fresh, despite the knockdown, and went to work on Cooper. The Englishman's face was a mask of blood from numerous cuts above his eyes. The referee stopped the fight. Ali was still unbeaten, untied, and on his way to a world championship fight with Liston.

85

It Takes
All Kinds

It wasn't easy keeping boxing going in the Garden through the 60's. By 1964, Ali was the world heavyweight champion and overshadowed the other weight classes. And he was fighting everywhere but in the Garden. That was bad enough, but then the house really fell in. Gillette had cancelled its contract to televise our fights. We had the Nigerian middleweight, Dick Tiger, scheduled with Don Fullmer, Gene's brother, in Cleveland on September 11, 1964. "Gillette's finished after that," Markson told me.

We had been connected with Gillette for so long, nobody ever thought the deal would end. When it did, we were forced to think in a different way about putting fights into the Garden. With TV you were assured of money up front, which helped pay for the fighter's services. Without the TV money, we had to think of drawing money at the gate. And there just weren't enough attractive matches around to assure a profit.

Besides, the people who had taken over in the Garden after Norris got heaved out had big plans. They made a deal with the Pennsylvania Railroad to build a new Madison Square Garden above Penn Station, down in the garment district of New York City. The deal involved maybe $100 million. The thought of supplying fights for the new arena kept me up nights. Muhammad Ali was on my mind all the time.

He was still being handled by the Louisville Sponsoring Group, but he was now an open Black Muslim and under the influence of Elijah Muhammad's Nation of Islam. In 1966, he defended his title five times. Four of them were outside the United States. He was talking out more and more about the war in Vietnam, saying he "ain't got no argument with them Vietcong." It was wiser for him to fight in Europe.

He had a new manager. Herbert Muhammad, Elijah Muhammad's son, had taken over after Ali's contract with the Louisville Sponsoring Group expired. The parting was peaceful. Nobody called anybody names. I knew Herbert and liked him a lot. He seemed a soft, easy-going guy, but when you had to make a deal with him he could be pretty tough. And he was pretty cute. Not only did he manage Ali, but he owned a piece of Ali's promotions, through a company called Main Event.

Main Event was the corporate handle of Bob Arum, a young New York lawyer; Mike Malitz, who had worked with his father, Lester M. Malitz, on the closed-circuit TV of the Ali-Jones bout; Jimmy Brown, the former Cleveland Browns running back; John Ali, a Black Muslim with an eye for new business, and Herbert Muhammad.

Arum came into the picture through Mike Malitz. They were neighbors in an apartment house on East 77th Street in Manhattan; and Arum, while serving as an assistant U. S. attorney in the Southern District of New York and later in the office of Louis Nizer, had handled some matters for the Malitzes. He was a bright guy—a graduate of Harvard Law School—and absolutely tireless. He would work twenty-four hours a day to put a deal across. I think Main Event, Inc., was his deal. Brown was in be-

88

cause he was a black sports hero who had some clout with Herbert Muhammad.

When I first heard about Main Event, Inc., I didn't think much of it. But pretty soon I realized we were up against tough competition. It isn't easy to do business with a fighter if his manager also wants to promote his fights.

Ali fought five fights for Main Event, Inc., in 1966 and 1967. He knocked out Henry Cooper in a return bout in London; almost drowned in the same city when Brian London caused a tidal wave in three rounds; finished off Karl Mildenberger in twelve rounds in Frankfurt, Germany; destroyed Cleveland Williams in three rounds in the Houston Astrodome, and went back to the same arena to punish Ernie Terrell for fifteen rounds.

I got mad. I went to see Herbert Muhammad and raised a beef. Couldn't we get Ali for one fight? The word out of Houston, where Ali's draft board was located, was that he would soon be asked to step forward and accept membership in the Army. We wanted him for the Garden before that happened.

I knew Herbert was hooked into the Main Event bunch, and I told him so. What I did was to romance him. I don't mean I flattered him. He was too smart for that. But he kind of got the idea that I liked him and found him a square-shooter.

Finally, he said to me, "Teddy, show me a deal where we can make some money, and you got Ali." I offered him a match with Zora Folley. "I can pay you $275,000," I said. In the fight before Ali had received $585,000 against Terrell.

"Don't sound like much," Herbert said. "Ain't half as much as we got fighting Terrell."

"Ain't the same kind of match," I said. "Folley's been around fifteen years and ain't got much left. Ali'll play with him."

"Ain't a lot of money," Herbert said.

"It's the best we can do," I said.

Herbert Muhammad took the match and Ali knocked out

Folley in the seventh round. It's a funny thing, Folley drowned a few years later in a pool in Chandler, Arizona, where he lived. I always wondered about his death. He seemed to be an awfully good swimmer when he fought Ali.

That bout took place on March 22, 1967. It was the last world championship fight in the old Garden. But it was historic for another reason, I think. It was Ali's last fight before he refused to step forward to be inducted into the U.S. Army. On April 28, 1967—I'll never forget the date—the New York State Athletic Commission revoked Ali's license as a fighter. With it went the heavyweight title. It took him seven years to get it back.

It didn't take long for the plotting to begin. What the hell, in boxing the referee always says, "Protect yourself at all times." It's the same outside the ring as inside. We made some moves to make sure we weren't out in the cold.

About that time we heard news that worried us. It was that Bob Arum and ABC-TV were organizing a tournament to get a new heavyweight champion. I said Arum was a guy who worked twenty-four hours a day. He does, and as soon as Ali lost his recognition as the world champion, the wheels in Arum's brain started spinning.

The first thing he did was to go to the World Boxing Association and get approval for a world heavyweight championship tournament. Then he sold it to the network people, but before he could do that he had to make a move in connection with Main Event, Inc., the company in which Herbert Muhammad and John Ali had a piece. He cut them out and formed a new corporation—Sports Action, Inc. The stockholders were Arum, Malitz, Jimmy Brown and Fred Hofheinz, who later became the mayor of Houston. Hofheinz's father, Roy, had been the brainchild behind the Houston Astrodome. The son was a wheeler-dealer, a big man down in Texas.

We got lucky. When Arum organized his tournament, he got eight major heavyweights to enter, including Jimmy Ellis, who, like Ali, was a native of Louisville, Kentucky. He also had some other good people in the competition, including Jerry Quarry, Floyd Patterson, Oscar Bonavena, Karl Mildenberger, Thad Spencer, and Ernie Terrell. Joe Frazier also was invited to take part.

I asked Yancey Durham, Frazier's manager, to come up from Philadelphia and offered him a fight with George Chuvalo, a tough Canadian heavyweight. Chuvalo's manager, Irving Ungerman, had refused to let his boy fight in Arum's tournament.

"We accept," Durham said. I wasn't surprised. Durham—we all called him "Yank"—was an old fight guy who knew how to make a fighter and make a buck. He got lucky with Frazier and made a lot of money.

When Yank accepted the Chuvalo fight for Frazier, I breathed easier because that meant he would not go into Arum's tournament. "You don't need the tournament," I told Yank. "You go into it you got to fight three times to get the title. And if you win it, there will be seven losers, and who are you going to fight?"

"Man, you been readin' my mind," Durham said. He had a booming voice and when he spoke the walls shook. The walls in the old Garden shook that day. "We ain't gonna go into no tournament," Durham said. I could hear the words bounce off a wall. Frazier stayed out and fought Chuvalo. What a job he did on the Canadian. By the fourth round, Chuvalo's face poured blood. The referee stopped it. It was a big win for Frazier. In seventeen fights, he had knocked out fifteen. Nobody could deny that he was one of the best heavyweights in the world. I thought he was the best.

Around that time, Markson said, "Teddy, you better start thinking about a big show for the new Garden. It's going to open next March and Irving Mitchell Felt wants us to have a show that'll fill the place for the opening."

"I got some ideas," I said.

"So have I," Markson said.

Markson was a very smart fight guy. Like I said, he really

didn't belong in the business, but so long as he was in it, he worked very hard at doing the best job anybody could. He was a graduate of Union College in Schenectady, New York, and anybody who knows anything about colleges, knows Union as one of the best smaller colleges in the country. Besides, Markson read books and listened to good music. More than once he was caught at Carnegie Hall listening to classical music. This is the kind of guy that I had to work with, an absolutely, positively dead honest guy.

Despite this, we got along, and when we put our heads together to settle a problem, we usually came up with the right answers. This time Markson said, "We got to use Frazier on the opening show of the new Garden."

I agreed because it was obvious. What were we going to do with Frazier? Arum's heavyweight tournament was in progress and we obviously had to look in another direction. I came up with the answer. "How about Frazier and Buster Mathis for the heavyweight title?" I asked.

"Will anybody buy it?" Markson said.

"If we can sell it to the New York State Athletic Commission," I said, "we'll sell it to the public."

"Good, but not good enough," Markson said. "How would it go if we put Frazier and Mathis on a card with Griffith and Benvenuti?"

"We can make it," I said. It was a hell of an idea.

Nino Benvenuti was an Italian middleweight from Rome who had taken Griffith's middleweight title in the Garden in April 1967. What an upset that was. It caused so much excitement, we put Griffith and Benvenuti together at Shea Stadium five months later. This time Griffith got the decision in fifteen rounds. Though the rubber match was a natural, it still wasn't big enough to stand on its own to open the new Garden.

"We'll make it a double-header," Marson said. "Two title fights."

92

When Markson went down to see Eddie Dooley, the chairman of the New York Boxing Commission, he found a friendly ear. Dooley said he would recognize the winner of a fight between Frazier and Mathis as the heavyweight champion.

At first this sounded good, but the more we thought of it, the more we realized that the title wouldn't mean anything if only the New York State Athletic Commission recognized it. The Frazier-Mathis fight needed more support.

It was true that the fight made some sense just as a fight. Frazier and Mathis had fought before—as amateurs. Mathis qualified to represent the United States in the Tokyo Olympics in 1964 by beating Frazier in the final qualifying bout. In training, however, Mathis hurt his hand and Frazier subbed as our heavyweight in Tokyo and won an Olympic gold medal.

Now they were both pros, and both were undefeated. Frazier weighed almost 200 pounds, but Mathis, who was closer to 250, towered over him. People thought Mathis, who was very fast on his feet, could move around enough to take a decision in fifteen rounds. I liked Frazier because he moved in all the time and threw hundreds of punches in a fight without taking any backward step.

Anyway, Markson came up with a plan. For a straight guy, he knew a lot about schemes. He would have made a pretty good general, except that he went in for culture instead.

"I got it, I got it," he said to me one day. "You know John Cronin up in Boston. He knows Ed Urbec, the chairman of the Massachusetts Boxing Commission. If Cronin can get Urbec to go along with New York in recognizing the Frazier-Mathis winner as champion, we'll look a little better."

I knew Cronin. He was a lawyer who had been involved with Paul Pender when Pender won a piece of the middleweight title from Sugar Ray Robinson in 1960.

"See what Cronin can do," I said.

Cronin did very well. In a few days we got word that

Massachusetts would go along with New York on Frazier and Mathis. Still Markson worried. "Not enough, not enough," he said every day. "We need more." Cronin had connections in England. We made a trip to London and got the British Boxing Board of Control to do something for us. The board announced publicly that before anybody else could be recognized as the successor to Muhammad Ali, he would have to fight the winner of the Frazier-Mathis bout.

Good, but no cigar. Markson was still worried. He got in touch with two fight guys in Chicago—Irving Schoenwald, a promoter, and Ben Bentley, a real good press agent out there. They got Illinois to go along with New York.

We tried Pennsylvania next and thought we'd have no trouble because Frazier was from Philadelphia. We had trouble. Pennsylvania was tied up with the WBA and as a member of the association was committed to recognizing the winner of Arum's tournament.

On March 4, 1968, the new Garden opened its doors for a sports event for the first time. Every seat in the new arena was occupied and the 18,096 customers paid a gross gate of $658,503. The night was a huge success, if I say so myself. Benvenuti took the middleweight title from Griffith on a close decision. Mathis outboxed Frazier for ten rounds, but Smokin' Joe caught him in the eleventh and knocked him out. The next month Jimmy Ellis, Ali's neighbor in Louisville, won the WBA title by beating Quarry in fifteen rounds.

Looking back on all that, I got to think we were pretty lucky. Both Frazier and Ellis were dead-honest fighters who got where they were by fighting dead-honest fights. When I think of that, I remember something that still bothers me.

About this time I kept hearing about a Basque heavyweight named José Urtain. He had a long string of knockout victories on his record and people in boxing were beginning to talk about him as a "white hope." I never went for this white hope

94

business, because to me a fighter is a fighter regardless of color. Would it matter if Joe Louis were white, or Sugar Ray Robinson? I know of no better man than Joe Frazier and to me Muhammad Ali is about as great as they come.

I was curious about Urtain, however, and I thought it would be nice to bring him to Madison Square Garden for a fight. International matches have always had a special flavor in boxing. Nowadays it is common for foreign fighters to campaign in the United States, even bad foreign fighters. Television brought that about, but years ago only the good foreign fighters came to this country for work.

I said to Markson one day, "Harry, I think it would be a good idea if I went to Madrid to see this Urtain fight. He's fighting an American heavyweight and I could get a line on him." He said I should go.

In Madrid the local promoter met me at the airport and treated me like royalty. The name "Madison Square Garden" means a lot in boxing throughout the world and just to be affiliated with the Garden puts a guy in the upper crust of boxing.

The day after I got to Madrid the promoter gave a luncheon in my honor at the best hotel in town. I got up and made a little speech. I said I wanted to match Urtain with Floyd Patterson in Madison Square Garden and that was why I was in town. The promoter got up and made a speech saying that my visit was a great tribute to Spain and to Spanish boxing, and how happy they would be to see Urtain fight in Madison Square Garden.

The next night I went to the fight and walked into the dressing room of the American fighter. I knew him from back in New York and I said, "Look, I've come a long way to see this Urtain. I want to see how good he is or how bad he is. But first I want to know one thing. Is this fight on the level?"

The American looked at me and said, "Mr. Brenner, they want me to fall down in three rounds." I asked him, "What are you going to do?" He said, "I don't know. They threaten about

95

not paying me if I don't do it. I don't know what to do." He was a kid out of a black ghetto who had never been in Europe before and was scared to death.

"Well, I'm going to tell you what to do," I said. "You do your best. Go out and fight your best. Don't worry whether they're going to pay you or not, and don't worry about them threatening you any harm, because that's not going to happen. I didn't come three thousand miles or four thousand miles to watch this guy fight an American fighter who is going to take a dive."

"Sure glad you came, Mr. Brenner," the American fighter said.

"I'll protect you in whichever way I possibly can," I said.

"I'm going out there and knock him out," the American said.

He went out, didn't throw a punch for two rounds and, in the third round, got slapped on the side of the head and went down. He rolled over and made it seem that they could have counted to a hundred in Spanish without waking him.

I don't want anybody to get the impression that things like the tank job in Madrid are restricted to European boxing. Hell, no. We have plenty of it going on in the United States. The only point I want to make is that when an American fighter gets to the top—at least in the time of Frazier and Ali—he has made the climb the hard way.

I have more proof of this. One time I was in London with Joe Louis and our friend Robbie Margolies. We were walking down Piccadilly when we ran into an American heavyweight named Billy Daniels. He had been in with the best of them, including Muhammad Ali when "The Greatest" was still called Cassius Clay. They fought for me at St. Nick's and the fight was stopped because Daniels had a cut over his eye, though Clay's eye was also cut.

Now, in London, Daniels was scheduled to fight a sensational Englishman named Billy Walker. Walker was a spectacular gate attraction and it would have been a shame to see him lose, not when he was drawing big crowds and getting good reports in the English press.

When we met Daniels in Piccadilly, I said to him, "You in good shape?"

"Oh, pretty good shape," he said.

Right away I knew something was wrong. "You going to lick this guy tomorrow?"

"I don't know. They don't want me to win," he said.

"Who doesn't want you to win?"

"The people that brought me over," the American said. "They told me I got to lose."

Joe Louis looked at him and said, "Listen, you don't have to lose to anybody. You go out and do your best and just don't worry about what people say they're going to do to you. If you can beat Walker, beat him. He ain't no better man than you if you can beat him."

"I don't know, I don't know," Daniels said.

When we left him he seemed absolutely bewildered. The next day he took a plane back to New York without going through with the fight. It takes all kinds.

Out of the Doghouse and Into the Garden

Ali was in the doghouse for three years. They gave him five years for draft evasion, but even while the case was on appeal he couldn't get a license anyplace. Bob Arum tried to get a match for him in Canada. The U.S. wouldn't let him leave the country. The Black Muslims bitched to high heaven about that.

I felt sorry for Ali. I liked him and he was taking a bum rap, while Frazier, the Garden's heavyweight champion, and Ellis, the WBA champion, were picking up nice checks fighting in defense of their titles. I knew that there would not be a real champion until Ali got back into action, but we kept pushing Frazier at the Garden.

He won four fights and then I went after Ellis. I wanted a "unification fight" between Frazier and Ellis. That way we would have only one champion to put in with Ali if he beat the draft rap.

Ellis was managed by Angelo Dundee, whose brother Chris was the boxing promoter in Miami Beach. As soon as Chris heard we were talking about putting Frazier in with Ellis, I heard from him. I wasn't surprised.

"Hey, Teddy," Chris Dundee said, "I hear you're working on Frazier and Ellis. I just want you to know I got a contract for Ellis to defend his title in Miami Beach."

"You got what?" I said.

"Listen, it's not my fault," Chris said. "I got the contract and what are you going to do about it?"

What I did was scream. "You got a contract for Ellis to fight in Miami Beach? Let me tell you something. I just looked at Ellis's record. He never fought a single fight in Miami Beach. How come now, when we want him for Frazier, you suddenly got a fight for him in Miami Beach? It stinks."

I went to Harry Markson and told him about our problem. "What's it going to cost us?" he asked. We had been through this sort of thing before. Other promoters came to us from time to time, when we were trying to make certain matches, to tell us they had the fighters booked and stood to get hurt if we broke up their bouts. We paid off.

Markson and Chris Dundee reached an agreement. "How much did he get us for this time?" I asked Markson, who raised both hands, palms out. "Ten," Markson said. "Cheap," I said. We were paying Frazier and Ellis $300,000 each for the fight. Giving Chris Dundee $10,000 wouldn't hurt us.

Thirteen days before the fight, Ali called a press conference. He announced that he was through with fighting, even if he won his case against the government, and offered his championship belt to the winnner of the Frazier-Ellis fight. It was a grandstand play. Frazier turned down the offer. "Don't need that man's belt," he said. "When I fight Clay, I'll give him my belt—on the nose." He insisted on calling Ali "Clay."

Frazier knocked out Ellis in five rounds. That stung Ali, who was Ellis's friend. When they were both amateur fighters in

Louisville, Ellis beat Ali. Frazier's win put a lot of respect into Ali.

In June 1970, the Supreme Court reversed Ali's conviction on the ground that, as a Black Muslim, he was a conscientious objector on religious grounds. I knew it wouldn't be long before he started boxing again. They made a match for him in Atlanta with Jerry Quarry and we all went down there to see Ali's return to the ring. But I didn't go with an empty mind. I had an offer to make to Ali if he beat Quarry.

He didn't have an easy time with Quarry, even if the fight went only three rounds. Quarry got cut pretty bad and his corner couldn't stop the blood, so the fight was halted. There wasn't enough fighting to tell us if Ali had anything left after the three-year layoff.

The hotel we all stayed in was the Hyatt Regency in Atlanta. After the fight I saw Ali in the lobby. It was about three o'clock in the morning. Ali was talking to a girl who must have weighed two hundred pounds. She wasn't just ugly. She was pretty ugly. Pretty soon, the girl went up the elevator and Ali followed her.

An hour later he was back in the lobby. I said to him, "Hey, champ, I know where you were. You went to that girl's room. How could you? She was ugly, man, ugly."

Ali laughed. "You say that, Teddy, who's gonna believe you? Me with my pretty face and she with her ugly face, who's gonna believe I made it with her?"

The next day I talked to Herbert Muhammad about making a match between Ali and the Argentinean heavyweight Oscar Bonavena. "Sounds all right with me," the manager said. When I went after Bonavena, my old friend Chris Dundee was in action again. He had just put some new people in with Bonavena and the new managers had signed a contract for Bonavena to fight for Dundee. We had to pay Dundee more than $10,000 to get Bonavena for the fight with Ali. Like we say in boxing, never jam a hustler.

I wasn't surprised when I found out that Dundee was in the picture again. Doing business with Bonavena had always been a pain in the ass. What else was new?

A few years before, I had made a match between Bonavena and George Chuvalo, the Canadian heavyweight. Dr. Marvin Goldberg—he was one of those guys who fitted glasses on you—was Bonavena's manager then and when I asked him to fight Chuvalo, he said, "What can Oscar get for the fight? He wants $10,000 for himself."

"I can't guarantee him $10,000 for himself," I said. "He'll have to fight on percentage and he can get twenty percent."

"What'll you think the fight'll draw?"

"It'll do about $80,000," I said.

"Well, then he would get $16,000," Dr. Goldberg said. "After I take my cut, Oscar'll have $10,000 for himself."

"I think you're right," I said.

"In that case," Dr. Goldberg said, "I'll guarantee him the $10,000 and take my chances. You say we'll get $16,000. It's all right with me."

It came up pouring cats and dogs the day of the fight. It was still raining at dinner time. We had about 8,000 customers in the old Garden and maybe there was $35,000 in the till. I knew we were going to have trouble.

An hour or so before Bonavena and Chuvalo were to go into the ring, one of Bonavena's brothers called me on the phone. He was with Oscar in the Loew's Midtown Inn across from the old Garden.

"You better come over," the fighter's brother said. "There's trouble."

"Trouble?" I said. "What kind of trouble?"

"Oscar hurt his back."

I got soaked running through the rain to get to

Bonavena's room in the motel. Oscar was in bed in his underwear, moaning that his back was hurt and he could not fight. His brother and his lawyer were at his bedside.

"I can't fight," the fighter moaned. "My back's killing me."

I glared at him. I said, "You can't fight? There's nothing wrong with your back."

"I'm sick," the fighter said.

Now his brother took me into the john. He said, "The back really hurts Oscar, but if you give him $10,000 that he wants, his back will get better. You must bring the $10,000 here before he'll go across to the Garden."

"I'll get him the $10,000," I said. "I'll be right back."

I did not wait for the elevator. I rushed down the stairs, crossed the street to the Garden, and got Jack Fitzpatrick. He was the head box-office guy. I said, "Can you count out $5,000 in small bills? He started counting. I rushed out to the arena and got Frank Morris, who was the chief deputy commissioner of the New York State Athletic Commission. I told him the story.

"We're going back to the motel," I told him. "I'm going to bring $5,000 in a paper bag and we're going to hand the bag over to Bonavena or his lawyer. Let them start counting the money. It's going to take a long time to count it. When they get three-quarters through the money, you say, 'Now look, that's enough. I'm a member of the New York State Athletic Commission and I guarantee the contract. I guarantee that the money is right.'"

So we went upstairs. Bonavena started to count, and when he reached $3,800, I gave Morris the signal. On cue, he said, "All right, that's enough. It's getting late. You got to go across the street. I guarantee the money."

Bonavena's lawyer said to the fighter, "That's all right. O.K., as long as the commission says it's O.K. You go and fight."

We crossed the street. It was still raining hard. Eighth Avenue was deserted. Bonavena went to his dressing room and pulled on his fighting gear. He beat Chuvalo, too, but when the money in the house was counted, his 20 percent of the net receipts came to $9,500. Dr. Goldberg insisted on taking his cut, which left the fighter with about $6,000.

Bonavena went berserk. He cursed everybody—the Garden, his manager, and Frank Morris, the man from the boxing commission. Morris screamed back. "Listen, you punk," he said. "You were the one who was deliberately breaking the contract that was on file with the commission. What you were trying to do was to extort $10,000 from Madison Square Garden but they wouldn't stand still for it."

The next day Bonavena came back to the Garden. He raged through the boxing department and threatened to tear the building down. He punched a hole in a plywood door and then left. A while later, he called me. "You good man, my friend, Teddy," he said. "You get me another fight." I never learned why his attitude had changed so suddenly.

Now it was four years later and I had Bonavena in with Ali. I didn't sleep nights. I was worried about what Bonavena would pull. Nothing happened. He got into good condition and took Ali into the fifteenth and last round. Then Ali caught him and knocked him out, and I saw dollar signs dancing on the ceiling of the Garden. The next fight had to be Frazier and Ali. I knew it was going to be a tough one. Like in all things, money would be the problem. It always is.

I remember once, years ago, Billy Graham was fighting Beau Jack in the Garden. While training, Graham broke the small finger on his left hand and had to pull out of the match. In those day, it was easy to get a sub if a fighter fell out. All a matchmaker did was to go to Stillman's Gym and see who was training. Then he'd pick one as a substitute and he was in business.

When Graham fell out of the match with Beau Jack, Terry Young substituted for him. Young was a tough guy from the East Side, in Rocky Graziano's old neighborhood and he was managed by Jackie Levine, who was a friend of mine. The day after the fight, which Young won, I met Jackie Levine in the Garden, where he had come to pick up Young's purse.

In those day, a manager would get paid with a Madison Square Garden check, which he would take down to the Garden box office to be cashed. I went to the box office with Levine and after he had cashed the check for Young's purse, he asked me to have some lunch.

"Naw, I'm gonna go home," I said.

Levine said, "Look, take a ride with me over to Terry Young's house. I want to give him his money. Then we'll go over and get something to eat, like in Ratner's."

I said, "Okay, I'll go."

So we went over to Terry Young's house. He lived in a five-story tenement on the East Side and we walked up the five floors to get to his flat. We found Terry in bed and he looked as if a truck ran over him. He was battered and bruised, it was that kind of fight with Beau Jack. Jackie Levine said to Terry, "How you feelin'?" The kid said, "I'm okay, I'm okay." He really didn't feel all right, but there is one thing I know about fighters. If they win, the pain isn't as great as when they lose. Besides, his end of the purse came to $14,000.

The manager reached into the bag he was carrying with all those thousands of dollars in it, all wrapped up in neat bundles. He threw the bundles on the bed. "Here's your money, Terry," he said, and Terry said, "Leave it there." "No, count it," Jackie Levine said. The fighter was annoyed. "I don't have to count it," he said. "Listen, you count it," the manager said. "Please count it."

So Terry Young took the first bundle of ten $100 bills. He started counting and when he finished counting, he jumped off the bed and, standing there in his underwear, grabbed Jackie

Levine by the lapels and screamed, "That's wrong!"

"What's wrong?" the manager said. He was loud, because the fighter had him by the lapels and was pulling him toward him, as if he wanted to let the air out of him.

"There's only ten hunnerd dollar bills in that bundle. You said there was a thousand dollars in that bundle. And there's only ten hunnerd dollars bills."

"That's all there's supposed to be," Levine said.

"Bullshit, there's twelve hunnerd dollar bills in a thousand," the fighter said.

I got into the act. "There's only ten in a thousand," I told Terry.

"You mind your fuckin' business," the fighter screamed. "I'm askin' my mother about this." He screamed for his mother and she came into the bedroom. She had this neighbor with her.

"How many hunnerd dollar bills in a thousand?" the fighter asked.

"I think there's ten," his mother said. "I think so."

The neighbor ran out the flat and pretty soon she came back with her son, who was maybe fourteen years of age. Terry Young said to the kid, "Hey, how many hunnerd dollars in a thousand?"

"Ten," the kid replied. "Only ten."

"No kiddin'?" the fighter said.

Fighters always have trouble with money. So do managers. When we decided at the Garden that we could pay Frazier and Ali $1,250,000 each to fight in the Garden in 1971, Harry Markson and I took the train down to Philadelphia one Sunday morning and got off at North Philadelphia. Joe Frazier's gymnasium was right across Broad Street from the station, so we just walked over and met Frazier and Yank Durham.

The reason we made it on a Sunday was that there weren't any fighters or managers in the gym and we could have our privacy with Frazier and his manager. We went into Frazier's office and sat down at a table. Each of us had a pad and pencil in front of him. We started to talk about how much money it was going to cost to get the Ali fight for the Garden.

I said to Durham, "Yank, you're going to make more money with this fight than you ever dreamed there is in the whole world. The Garden is prepared to give you $1,250,000 as a guarantee against a percentage of thirty-five percent. We're prepared to give the same deal to Ali."

Durham looked at me and then he looked at Markson, and he said, "We've been offered a guarantee of $2,500,000 each for the fight. Same for Ali."

"Who made the offer?" Markson asked.

"Jerry Perenchio," Durham said.

Harry and I knew about Perenchio. He was associated with Jack Kent Cooke, then owner of the Los Angeles Lakers and the Los Angeles Forum. We knew the offer was legitimate. Perenchio was a big man in show biz and Cooke a big man in sports. Nobody doubted that when they said Cooke would guarantee Frazier and Ali $2,500,000 each, they weren't talking through their hats, if they ever wore hats. But we weren't going to give up easy.

"Let me tell you about that offer." I told Durham. "What's wrong with it is that you'll get a guarantee, but no percentage of the gross. We're giving you a percentage. If this fight takes place and does what people say it will, you'll wind up getting six or seven million dollars on the percentage. The reason we got the guarantee at $1,250,000 is because so many things can happen, even snow in March, to cut the gate down. The gamble is that you're going to get $1,250,000 from us. You can't get less, but you'll get considerably more if everything goes the way we think it will. Come to think of it, $1,250,000 ain't bad."

Durham and Frazier each took a pencil and I said,

"Write down $1,250,000." They both started to write. Durham looked at Frazier's figure. He said, "You got a zero too many." Frazier said, "You got this little comma in the wrong place." Neither one could write the figures in $1,250,000 without making a mistake.

Finally, Durham said, "One thing I know, we're going to take $2,500,000. That's a lot more than $1,250,000, no matter how you write it. But one thing I'm telling Jack Kent Cooke and this Perenchio. The fight's got to take place in Madison Square Garden, no matter what else happens."

Durham kept his word. He told Bruce Wright, who was Frazier's lawyer, "No matter what happens with that Perenchio and that Cooke, we got to fight in the Garden, no place else. Don't care about nothing else."

Wright notified Perenchio of Durham's demand. "We'll take the fight on one condition," the lawyer notified Perenchio. "It has to take place in Madison Square Garden. We owe it to them. They've been very good to us."

The way it turned out, Frazier and Ali collected only $2,500,000 for their first fight. If they had taken the deal the Garden offered before Perenchio came into the picture—a guaranteed $1,250,000 or 35 percent, whichever was greater, they would have made about $6 million each.

The fight was a great success, both in the Garden and on closed-circuit TV. Tickets priced at $150 each were scalped on Broadway and in Harlem for $500 apiece. Hustlers got rich. In the saloons of Harlem, along Lenox Avenue and Seventh Avenue, scalpers somehow turned up with tickets that had been allocated to Frazier's and Ali's camps. People whispered that a lot of hangers-on in both camps got rich. The Garden made a comfortable profit. Perenchio and Cooke split millions. Frazier got the decision in fifteen rounds, knocking Ali down for a nine-count in the last round. Ali left the ring with his jaw blown up the size of a grapefruit, but not before Frazier told him, "You put up a great fight. You fought one hell of a fight. You one bad nigger. We both bad niggers. We don't do no crawling."

"Great night," Markson told me.

"Best we ever had," I said.

I think we even got a little bonus. We also got letters of congratulations from Irving Mitchell Felt, the chairman of the board.

A King
Comes to Call

When Ali fought Quarry in Atlanta, the flower of the black social whirl was there. They filled the lobby of the Hyatt Regency and the beautiful broads wore the skins of wild animals. In the hotel driveway their Cadillacs and Rolls-Royces had special paint jobs and lizard-skin upholstery. It was something new in boxing.

Then, when Frazier beat Ali in the Garden, they came out again, only more of them. Hustlers were everywhere—some, pimps, wearing white full-length coats over costumes of the brightest colors. The women were beautifully gowned and their companions wore custom-made threads. Boxing was changing.

I could sense it and I was not surprised when Don King came into the picture. King was operating out of Cleveland, where he had been in numbers before doing four years hard for manslaughter. Boxing is a very small community and nobody comes into it secretly. Even real tough guys who buy pieces of fighters or back promoters can't move in without people whisper-ing.

The first time I met King was in 1973. How it happened was that I made a match between Jerry Quarry and my old pal Oscar Bonavena. They were both in the heavyweight limelight and the match figured to bring a big crowd to the Garden. But a few weeks before the fight, Bonavena got hurt in training.

I got hold of Gil Clancy, who was managing Quarry, and told him the fight was off if I could not get a substitute for Bonavena. "Geez, Teddy," Clancy said, "don't call it off. Get somebody for Jerry. He's been in training for a month and has a lot of expenses. I'd hate to see you call the show off."

It wasn't easy to get another opponent for Quarry. The few good heavyweights around were busy. George Foreman had just upset Frazier in two rounds and was the new champion. These were exciting times in the heavyweight picture, so everybody was working and I was hard-pressed to get somebody worthwhile co fill in for Bonavena.

Come to think of it, a matchmaker never knows what he's got until the fighters he has matched are in the ring and throwing punches. Like the fighters themselves, he is always on edge, because he is never sure that both fighters will get through their training grinds in good shape and then put on a real good fight.

Fighters pull out of bouts for many reasons. They are prima donnas. I once had a boxer walk out of the dressing room in the Garden and shuffle off to Buffalo a couple of hours before he was supposed to fight. The reason he went to Buffalo was because that was where he lived. His name was Jimmy Ralston and I'll never forget him, not because he was much of a fighter but because of the tricks he pulled on me.

Ralston was a light-heavyweight who had never boxed in the Garden, though he was moving up in the 175-pound class. I thought he had the ability to become a light-heavyweight contender, and when José Torres was making a comeback after los-

112

ing the title to Dick Tiger, I made him with Ralston for the Garden.

I thought I was doing Ralston a favor, but when he got to New York a week before the fight he started to complain that he was not in the best condition. The day before the fight he came to me and said he was all right. The next day, he went to the State Athletic Commission offices and weighed in, and I breathed a sign of relief. That night he came to the Garden, went to his dressing room and sat around until about eight o'clock, two hours before he was scheduled to fight. Suddenly, he got up and walked out of the Garden. Don't think I ever saw him again.

Here we had about 8,000 customers in the arena and I didn't have a main event. I got hold of Duke Stefano, my assistant for more than twenty years, and I told him what happened. "What are we going to do, Duke?" I said.

Duke Stefano was one of the best guys I ever met in boxing. A little guy with a sense of humor, he also had a sense of loyalty. In all the years he worked for me I never had any reason to doubt him. He was one hundred percent for me. Now he said, "Teddy, I just saw Charlie Green sitting upstairs eating a hot dog. Maybe he'll fit in."

I rushed upstairs and found Green. I said, "Charlie, how do you feel?" He said, "I feel all right, Mr. Brenner." I said, "How'd you like to fight tonight?" He looked at me as if I had lost my marbles. "Something wrong?" he asked. I told him about Ralston. Then I offered him $5,000 to fill in for Ralston against Torres.

"The $5,000's all right," Green said, "but I paid six dollars for this ticket. And it's 65 cents for this hot dog I just ate. It's going to cost you six dollars and 65 cents plus $5,000 for me to fight Torres." I said, "Let me talk to Torres."

I went into Torres's dressing room and I explained what had happened. He knew Green because they had sparred in the gym. He said, "Give me five minutes to think about it." I left to tell the boxing commission about the problem and returned to Torres's dressing room in about ten minutes. Torres wasn't in the room. I waited for him. He came back in a few minutes and said everything was all right, he would take Green.

I rushed out and notified the boxing commission that the main event would go on. Then we made an announcement from the ring. There had been a last-minute substitution, we announced, and anybody who wanted a refund on his ticket could get it at the box-office. We did not have to refund one red cent.

The bell rang for the start of the first round. For two minutes nothing happened. Then Green, who was a very good puncher, let go with a vicious left hook, followed by a right to the head. Down went Torres. The crowd was screaming. He got up at nine. Green moved in with another left hook. It caught Torres's jaw. He went down again. The count reached four when the bell rang.

The referee did not know what to do. He was not used to a new rule in boxing that called for the count to continue after the bell if a fighter was on the floor when the bell sounded.

So Torres's seconds jumped into the ring, dragged him to his corner, and revived him. In the next round, Torres hit Green a hell of a shot. Green took it on the chin, went down and was counted out. Not a customer booed.

I went back to Green's dressing room. "Charlie," I said, "what happened?"

He looked at me and said, "What do you mean, what happened?"

I said, "Charlie, did he really hit you that hard?"

"Hard enough," Green said.

It's been a long way around, but what I meant when I started to tell you about the time I first met Don King was that a matchmaker never knows what he is going to get when he uses a substitute. And a lot of times he is lucky to get any substitute.

When Bonavena got hurt and pulled out of the fight with Quarry, I was in trouble. I checked all the available heavyweights. Finally, I came up with a name. Earnie Shavers was a heavyweight out of Ohio who was a devastating puncher, even if he did not take a punch well himself. He seemed like an ideal guy to fill in for Bonavena against Quarry. He had had only one fight in New York, a six-rounder, and the last I heard of him, he was being managed by Dean Chance. When he was with the Los Angeles Angels in 1964, Chance won the Cy Young Award as the foremost pitcher in major league baseball.

Chance was hustling boxers when I got to know him. He was a fast-talking guy who promoted fights around Cleveland and wound up managing fighters. He managed Shavers for a while, but when I suggested to Clancy that Shavers would make a good opponent for Quarry, the manager said, "Funny thing, when I was in Paris a few months ago for a fight, I met a guy there who said he was Shavers's new manager. A big, tall guy with wild hair and a lot of money in his kick. Boy, he could spend money. His name was Don King."

"Will you fight Shavers?"

"Sure, but he's a good puncher, Teddy," Clancy said. "If Quarry gets knocked out or loses, I want a return bout."

"I can't do that, I said. "You know the Garden can't get involved in return-bout contracts because of the antitrust decision."

"I know that," Clancy said, "but maybe we can work something out."

So I put in a call for Don King in Cleveland and introduced myself. "Is Shavers available to fight Quarry?" I asked King. "Would he like to fight him?"

"Would he!" King answered, and his voice came booming into my ear. "If we get that shot, I'll never be able to thank you in a million years. You're giving me a chance I didn't think I'd ever get with Shavers."

When King arrived in my office in Madison Square Garden, he must have been surprised. At the time, the Garden boxing department—Madison Square Garden Boxing, Inc.—was hidden away in the catacombs of the new arena. Later, when they were getting ready for the 1976 Democratic Convention in the Garden, the boxing department was moved upstairs, like the spy who came out of the cold, to make way for a police command post. But when King first stepped into my office, he found it a windowless, drab room. His gaudy clothes lit up the place.

We talked for a while and he gave me a demonstration of his bullshit—the booming voice, the black hair standing on end as if it had been shocked and forgot to relax, the diamond rings on his fingers and the smile that never seemed to leave his face. He was something else.

"I'm going to give you $12,500 for Shavers to fight Quarry," I said.

"That's fair," King said.

I said, "Don, Madison Square Garden can't sign a fighter for two fights, but if Shavers should win, Quarry would like to box him again and I'd like you to tell me that you agree. What I will guarantee you is that the least you will get for a second fight with Quarry, if Shavers should win the first, would be $25,000."

"You know you got me, Teddy," King said. "You don't have to ask me. You just go ahead and do what you want."

A few days later Quarry got sick. He had a cold or something, and couldn't fight, and I called King and told him that we were in trouble. "Please, please, Teddy, don't call off the fight. Get somebody else for Shavers," King pleaded.

Then I told the Garden people about Quarry getting sick. They told me to go ahead and get a substitute, because the fight would be shown on cable TV and that would be the first time for this kind of telecast from the Garden. It was going to be coast-to-coast.

So I called Don King and said, "Look, I can get Jimmy

Ellis to fight Shavers. He used to be the world heavyweight champion and still means something."

"No problem here," King said. "Go ahead."

I got in touch with Angelo Dundee in Miami. He was handling Ellis even though he was working with Muhammad Ali. He couldn't see why Ellis couldn't get ready to fight Shavers. It was a payday, wasn't it? Managers eat better when fighters fight.

We made Ellis with Shavers, and it turned out to be a one-round fight. At the opening bell, Ellis came out and hit Shavers on the chin with his right hand. Shavers was wobbly and it looked like the fight was going to end right then and there. When Ellis rushed in to finish Shavers off, he was met instead by a right hand to the chin. Down he went and the referee counted him out. Shavers was a big hit in the Garden.

The next day, Don King showed up in my office. I said, "Don, can we make the Jerry Quarry fight now?" He said, "Oh, that'd be fine." And I said, "Remember what I told you? I said if you beat Jerry Quarry, when we made a return your starting point would be $25,000." "I remember what you told me," King said. "But now, if you want the Jerry Quarry fight, the starting point is not going to be $25,000. It's going to be a lot more than $25,000."

I came off my chair. I was mad. I said, "Don, remember what you said. You said, 'Do anything you want, it'll be all right.' You knew we couldn't sign you for two fights because of the antitrust decree, but I thought we could take you at your word."

He smiled. His teeth were sharp. He said. "There's no way I'm going to let Shavers fight for $25,000."

"But you gave me your word, Don," I said.

"If you want the fight I want $50,000 guaranteed, against a percentage."

My blood pressure went up. I knew he had me. The court

had put handcuffs on the Garden and King was taking advantage of our situation. But he was not keeping his word. I said, "Don, I've got to talk to Harry Markson and Ned Irish. I'll get back to you."

When I went to see Ned Irish, who was president of the Garden, Markson accompanied me to his office. He knew about King's tactics. I told Irish that King was trying to hold us up and he asked, "How much will the fight draw?"

"About $200,000 net, I think," I said. "If Shavers gets twenty-five percent, it would come to $50,000 anyway. But we'll have to draw $200,000 for the percentage to equal the guarantee."

"Be prepared to give him what he wants, but try to get King to take less," Irish said.

Markson and I went down to our offices and King was in the boxing department. I went to work on him, but he wouldn't budge. "It's $50,000 or no fight," he said. I surrendered.

The fighters went into training and pretty soon I heard that Shavers was having wars in the gym with one of King's other fighters, a hard-hitting former jailbird named Jeff Merritt. I thought, Geez, that Merritt is a murderous puncher and Shavers is a murderous puncher, and if they let go in the gym, somebody's going to get hurt. So I got in touch with King and I warned him. I said, "Don, I've been around boxing a lot longer than you. I hear Earnie is boxing with Jeff Merritt and that's no good, because Merritt can knock your head off and somebody's going to get hurt."

"No, no," King said. "They're just going to work for a few more days and then Archie Moore says he'll separate them."

"I know Archie Moore very well," I said. "I knew him as a fighter and I know him as a trainer, and he is very good. But I hope he knows what he's doing in this case. I'm warning you, Don."

The next day King came into my office. His face was

down to the floor. He said, "Teddy, I got bad news. Merritt hit Shavers on the chin and broke his jaw. You'll have to call the fight off."

Now my face was down to the floor. "Oh, my God," I said, and he said, "Not only that. The doctor says Shavers won't be able to fight for at least four months."

"You didn't listen to my advice," I said.

"I listened to Archie Moore instead," King said.

"And look what happened."

He looked as if he was going to cry.

I started looking for somebody to fight Quarry. Nobody was available, so I thought, What the hell, I might as well just go for the big one. I tried to make Quarry with George Foreman for the world heavyweight championship. Foreman had won the title by knocking out Joe Frazier in Kingston, Jamaica, in two rounds and had knocked out a hambone named Joe Roman in one round in his first defense of the championship. Foreman wouldn't take the match.

When King heard I was going after Foreman for Quarry, he called me on the phone almost every day. "Don't make Quarry with Foreman," he pleaded. "Save Quarry for us."

"Why, Don?" I asked.

"Because if I don't get Quarry when Earnie's jaw is healed, everybody will forget about Shavers and his knockout of Ellis. Please don't break up our match with Quarry."

I said, "Listen, Don, I remember when you told me that $25,000 was the price when I first told you about Quarry. Then you knocked out Ellis and you jacked the price up to $50,000. I couldn't hold you to the $25,000 because I wasn't allowed to sign a fighter for two fights, and you took advantage of the anti-trust decree. And you asked for $50,000 to fight Quarry, instead of $25,000, and we gave it to you. Then Shavers got hurt. You know, Don, I don't think I owe you anything."

As King's luck would have it, I tried every way I knew

how to get another opponent to fight Quarry. I couldn't, and when Shavers finally got his doctor's permission to start training again, I went to King and we signed new contracts for the fight with Quarry. Only instead of giving King a $50,000 guarantee for Shavers's services, I gave him 25 percent without a guarantee.

I told King, "You went back on your word and now I want to give you only twenty-five percent for the Quarry fight. It is the same percentage you were getting before, only now people have probably forgotten Shavers and how he knocked out Ellis in one round."

King said, "You're taking advantage of me."

"Me? I'm taking advantage of you? Listen, when you had your shot, you took it. Now it's my turn. I think I'm giving you a fair proposition. You're not getting less money. Only this time you'll have to draw it. If the fight draws well, and I think it will, you may get more, but you'll get what your fighter draws."

King signed the contract for 25 percent of the net gate and Shavers went into training. Archie Moore no longer was handling Shavers and he was not sparring with Jeff Merritt.

We gave a luncheon for newspapermen at the Playboy Club in Manhattan. Both Quarry and Shavers showed up, and King came all decked out in a green tuxedo. The sun was shining outside, but he came in a tuxedo anyway. It was the first time he was on display in New York.

He made a speech about how the weight of the children of Ohio were on Shavers's shoulders, how they looked up to their Buckeye neighbor. "I don't have to listen to this shit," Quarry said, and he walked out.

In the Garden ring, Quarry went right to Shavers and took a shot before delivering his own bomb. He knocked out Shavers in one round. I went to Quarry's dressing room and congratulated him. Then I went into Shavers's room, where there was nothing but gloom. King saw me come in and and came running toward me. He said, "Teddy, Teddy, you must help me, please. Get me another fight for Earnie. You're the only one who can help me."

"Help you with whom?"

"With Earnie," he said, and I said, "Earnie? Earnie who?"

Shavers's 25 percent on the net gate came to $57,000.

14

They Can't Spell Gratitude

Don King never forgot what I said after Shavers was knocked out by Quarry. Whenever he could take a shot at me, he took it. I wasn't bothered because I was a boxing man through and through and he was a Johnny-come-lately.

To me a boxing man is a guy who has been in the game and has "made" fighters. By that I mean he has taken a kid out of the amateurs and brought him along. Or, if he's a matchmaker, he knows how to put two fighters together in the ring and get a contest out of them.

The way fighters are made today is another story. Television calls the shots. This is not bad when the TV people know what they are doing, but when they have no matchmaker to guide them, they are in trouble. The way they work is to get a "star" attraction on one side of a match and then throw the other guy to the wolves. That's not matchmaking.

I've heard certain people say I must have been drunk when I made a certain match. The trouble with that is that I don't drink, not even to be sociable. But I have made some bad matches. I even made one match I didn't want to make, and I can't forget it. Why it keeps bothering me I don't know. Nobody is perfect, even if he stays in his job as matchmaker at the Garden for twenty years. But there's one goddamn thing I know, and that is that nobody knows more about how to make a match than I do.

I remember the time I was trying to make Jerry Quarry and Mac Foster for the Garden. This was in 1970 and Foster was big in boxing. He was a former Marine who had knocked out twenty-four guys in a row and was the hottest attraction in California. He was managed by Pat DiFuria, who I knew because he had handled a California light-heavyweight by the name of Wayne Thorton when I used Thorton in the old Garden.

DiFuria knew that Quarry and Foster was a hell of a match. What he also knew was that the fight belonged in California, not in New York. I think he even gave his word to Eileen Eaton, who was promoting in Los Angeles, that he would fight for her. I knew it was going to be tough to make the match, but I kept after DiFuria. I'd call him during the day and then at night, and pretty soon he started to cringe when he heard my voice on the phone.

The pressure I put on him was too much for him. He called Markson from the West Coast and said, "Harry, I don't want to talk to Brenner. He's putting too much pressure on me, but everything he says makes sense and I can't argue with him. He's too logical. If I'm going to make Foster with Quarry, I'll have to do business with you."

When Markson told me about DiFuria's call, I laughed, because I knew he was weakening. I wanted the match so badly I could taste it. Mrs. Eaton was screaming in California. She was threatening to sue the Garden if we put on the fight, but nothing ever came of it. We made the match and Foster couldn't handle the assignment. Quarry knocked him out in six rounds. Pat DiFuria was done in by logic.

If I had stuck to logic I would never have made the fight for the world light-heavyweight championship between Bob Foster and Frank DePaula. That was a match I did not want, did not need, and worried a lot about. It was the only match I ever made that was not competitive.

DePaula was a rough kid from over in New Jesey who could not fight very much but was very exciting because he kept throwing punches and usually knocked people out. When I put him in with Dick Tiger in the Garden, he made a hell of a showing. It was one of the best fights we ever had in the arena and everybody was talking about DePaula, even though he lost the fight. Tiger was a brave man who held both the middleweight and light-heavyweight titles and the fact that DePaula almost handled him made the Jersey puncher a big favorite.

So now, one day, I'm sitting in my office in the Garden and in comes Willie Gilzenberg. If you remember, he's the guy I followed into Laurel Gardens in Newark when I was promoting in Jersey, after almost choking Al Weill for putting a fast one over on me. Now we were friends. Gilzenberg had gone into the promotion of wrestling and had an office in the Garden. But this day, when he came into my office, he was on boxing business.

"There are people trying to make DePaula and Foster for the title over in Jersey," Gilzenberg said. "Only thing stopping it, is me. I can stop it from going over there if you want the match. They'll step aside."

Gilzenberg's concern with my welfare was sudden and surprising. He was never known for being a charitable guy. It was hard to know when he was playing you for a sucker or playing it straight. I told him, "Willie, I know the match will draw a lot of money, but I don't want it. DePaula doesn't have a chance."

"It's going to be made," Gilzenberg said, "if not by you or me, by somebody else. Why should it get away from you?" I thought about it for a minute or two, but before I could answer, Gilzenberg said, "Look, Teddy, the people who run the Garden, like Irving Mitchell Felt, will want to know why you didn't make the match if it goes over to Jersey. Save yourself a lot of trouble. Make it."

I walked into Markson's office and told him about my talk with Gilzenberg. After all, Markson was my boss and I had to have him approve everything I did if it was important. Making a match for Madison Square Garden was the most important thing I could do.

"What do you think of a fight between Foster and DePaula?" I asked.

"It's a ridiculous match," Markson said.

"I'm glad you said that," I said. "Foster hits too hard. He's lanky and his left hook is as good as any in the business. I don't want to make the match."

"What I would suggest," Markson said, "is that we let Mr. Felt know about it. I'll get in touch with him." He did, and when he told Felt about the chance that Foster and DePaula would be made in New Jersey, Felt asked, "Why doesn't Teddy make it?"

"Because he thinks it's a bad match," Markson said. "So do I. DePaula doesn't have a chance and there's every likelihood that the boxing commission will not approve it."

"What I would do," Felt said, "would be to sign the fight and submit the contracts to the commission. If it's turned down we won't cry, but at least we will know that we tried. By the way, how much will it draw at the gate?"

When Markson said it would draw $200,000, Felt said, "Then we certainly should get after it." In 1969, $200,000 was maybe like a million-dollar gate today.

126

"I want to say one more thing, Mr. Felt," Markson said "I must tell you that Brenner knows a lot more about boxing than the commission, which is a political body. He has given his opinion, but if you think we should pursue the match, we'll make it."

So I made the match against my own judgment and, of course, it was approved by the commission, which was interested only in getting tax revenue for the state. We sold out the Garden and the gate receipts were more than $200,000. Foster toyed with DePaula, knocking him out in the first round with left hooks. I was ashamed of the whole thing. I left the Garden in disgust.

A few days later, DePaula came to my office. He said, "Look, Teddy, I'm worried. I lost to Dick Tiger and my manager gets me a shot at the light-heavyweight title. Knockout in one. Does that mean that the next guy I must fight is Joe Frazier for the heavyweight title?"

We laughed, and that was the last time I saw Frank DePaula. The next year he was found in an alley over in Jersey. Somebody had pumped his body full of bullets. It took him four months to die. I said he had guts.

DePaula could not fight much, but he had something that I always admired in fighters. A feeling that they were spcial people. In other things it is called professionalism. I'll tell you who had this thing I call professionalism. Joey Giardello. He was a middleweight from Brooklyn who fought out of Philadelphia and got to be world middleweight champion late in his career by beating Dick Tiger.

When he had the title, after sixteen years in the ring, a guy with a lot of money in his kick came to him and asked him to give a certain fighter a shot at the championship.

"The bum don't deserve it," Giardello said. "I can get you a lot of money for the fight," the hustler told Giardello, who got real mad. "Do you see this nose?" Giardello asked, placing his right forefinger there. "I got it flattened in tough fights with fellows like Henry Hank and George Benton. This cut over my eye I got from Sugar Ray Robinson, and my face ain't real pretty. Let your guy go out and fight real fighters and earn a shot, and then maybe I'll give him a chance at my title."

"But you'll get a bundle," the hustler insisted.

"Get going," Giardello said. Two fights later he lost the title to Dick Tiger.

Jake LaMotta had that pride of professionalism when he was leveling. The trouble was we never knew when he was square. What I remember about him most is the night he dumped to Blackjack Billy Fox in the old Garden. That night he had a fellow named Jimmy Remini in his corner. Remini didn't know what was going on, and when he saw LaMotta doing funny things in the first round, he couldn't believe his eyes.

When LaMotta came back to the corner at the end of the first round, Remini said, "Jake, Jake, what are you doing?" LaMotta looked at him and said, "What am I doing? Lissen, if I was you, I'd go out and hire myself a good lawyer."

I'm not trying to give the impression that all fighters and their managers are trustworthy. Because fighters are people, they act like anybody else. Most fight people can't spell the word gratitude. I gave Roberto Duran his first fight in the United States and then got him a shot at Ken Buchanan's lightweight title. He stopped Buchanan in the thirteenth round to become the world 135-pound champion, but he refused to give Buchanan a return bout. In fact, he never again fought a title bout for me in the Garden.

Duran's manager was a rich Panamanian named Carlos Eleta and we never hit it off. He told people in the Garden he did not trust me. What he meant is that he did not like to do business with me because I kept insisting that if Duran had an ounce of sportsmanship in him, he would have given Buchanan a return bout. He never did.

I gave George Foreman his first bouts after he won the gold medal in heavyweight boxing at the 1968 Olympic Games in Mexico City. He fought in the Garden nine times before he destroyed Joe Frazier in Jamaica in 1973 and won the world heavyweight championship. I never got him back in the Garden after that. Much worse, it was Foreman in a way who gave Don King the boost that made King a promoter. You'll see later that I have a damn good reason for remembering this.

15

Come Out, Come Out, Wherever You Are!

When Joe Frazier was offered a million or so to defend his heavy-weight title against George Foreman in Kingston, Jamaica, Yank Durham worried about the match. He knew Foreman could punch hard and warned Joe, "You ain't gonna have no picnic." But Frazier wanted the fight. So did Joe's lawyer, Bruce Wright, who ran the champion's company, Cloverlay, Inc.

I had talked first about the fight, but when I suggested it, Durham and Wright said there was a stumbling block. It in-volved money. There is one thing you can always depend on in boxing. If a problem comes up it usually involves money. In this case it went back to Frazier's first fight with Ali in the Garden, the one he got the title in and a purse of $2,500,000. From Joe's purse, the state of New York grabbed $315,000. Frazier claimed that he did not owe New York State that much in taxes, and he said he would never fight in the state until he got a refund.

When the Frazier-Forman match came up, I went to Markson and asked him if the Garden would be interested. He couldn't make a decision without talking to our bosses. When he did, he got a green light to deal with Frazier. But after talking to Durham and Wright, we realized that Frazier would cost the Garden almost $1,200,000. What Frazier wanted was for us to pay him the money withheld by the state of New York, in addition to a purse of $850,000. The Garden wouldn't go along with this.

About this time a fellow named Alex Valdez convinced the government of Jamaica that the promotion of a heavyweight championship bout in the capital, Kingston, would boost tourism on the island.

In New York, Hank Schwartz and Barry Burnstein ran a television facilities company called Video Techniques, which was involved mostly in closed-circuit telecasting for business conventions. Valdez went to see Schwartz and Burnstein and made a deal for Video Techniques to do the electronic pickup of the fight for closed-circuit TV in the United States.

Schwartz and Burnstein were not new to boxing. Nor was the name of Don King unfamiliar to them. They knew him as a small-time boxing promoter in Cleveland who had televised some minor bouts on a local closed-circuit basis. They had done business with him and when Frazier-Foreman was signed for Jamaica, Burnstein heard from King. "Like you to buy some tickets for me for the fight and get me a hotel room," King said. "You're in on the fight, so arrange it for me."

King went down to Jamaica and tried to give the impression he was tied in to the fight, which he wasn't. He was just a tourist, but he did not waste time. He began making time with Dick Sadler, Foreman's manager and trainer. They made an odd couple. Sadler was a little man who barely reached to King's mouth. He always had to hustle for a living, one way or another, and when he got his big break with Foreman, he was suddenly a big man in black society. He walked tall—all five feet four inches of him.

Foreman had one hero and that wasn't Sadler. He thought he resembled Sonny Liston most—as big and as strong as Liston, and, in his mind, as good a puncher. He was wrong, but that is what he believed. When he first told me that I laughed. I thought, hell, he couldn't last two rounds with Liston. Foreman wasn't mean enough to be a Liston.

Why I say this is that Sonny Liston was the meanest heavyweight champion of all. I remember hearing a story about the time he went to London, when he still had the title, to box a series of exhibitions on a tour arranged by Mickey Duff, an English promoter and manager.

Duff put Liston up in a fine hotel near Piccadilly Circus and three days before the first exhibition bout, the champion called the promoter. "Hey, what do I do today? This place is a morgue." Duff apologized. "Well, Sonny, it's Sunday and everything's closed today. Why don't you just relax?" Duff said.

"How about some broads?" Liston asked ·

"That's not my racket," Duff said. "I don't know what I can do to help you."

Duff went to a night club run by a friend. He told him about Liston's sudden need for companionship. "Hey, Mickey," Duff's friend shouted. A small girl—I think she was Scotch—answered. Duff's friend said to her. "You want to meet Sonny Liston?" "Wouldn't mind," the girl said.

Duff called Liston on the phone. "Sonny, there's a little girl here who would like to meet you," Duff said. "My friend here will send her over to the hotel. Maybe you'd better order some whisky and sandwiches from room service, so that it won't look suspicious you having a girl in your suite."

Within half an hour the girl named Mickey, accompanied by Duff and another man, arrived at Liston's suite. Liston looked at the girl and then at her companion. "Who's the fag she brought with her, Mickey?"

"No, no," Duff answered. "This fellow just came with

me. He's going to leave and then I'll leave, and I'll just see you tomorrow."

The next morning Duff invited two or three boxing writers to interview Liston in his suite. "Meet me in the foyer and
we'll go up together," Duff told the reporters. When they had as-
sembled, Duff escorted the reporters to Liston's floor. As they got
off the elevator, they heard a terrible argument going on in Liston's suite.

Inside, they found Liston wearing a robe that reached
just below his knees. The girl named Mickey was screaming,
"You bloody bastard! You bloody bastard!" Then, turning to
Duff, she said, "He fucked me all night. I got no sleep. And when
I was ready to leave, he gave me ten quid. Ten quid! Imagine."

Duff turned to Liston. "Sonny, that's only about twenty-
four dollars," he said.

"Yeah," Liston shouted, "and what about all the sandwiches she ate?"

That was Foreman's hero and I've got to say here that
Foreman fought like Liston the night he flattened Frazier in
Kingston. It was almost like Liston knocking out Patterson in
their two one-round fights, only it took Foreman two rounds to
take Frazier's title. All the action lasted only four minutes and
thirty-five seconds. Foreman had Frazier down six times, floor-
ing him with shots to the top of the head. I couldn't believe it.

When Foreman returned to his dressing room in the big
stadium in Jamaica, King was already there. He was operating.
Not only was he operating on Foreman and Sadler, but he was
moving closer to Herbert Muhammad, who was Muhammad
Ali's manager.

One thing everybody knew was that Ali was still the biggest attraction. I knew it, of course. That was why I matched him
for his second fight with Frazier in the Garden in 1974. I made it
for twelve rounds and we said it was for the American heavy-

weight championship. A sellout crowd saw Ali get the decision, but I thought Frazier had an edge. The referee let Ali hold too much.

Two months after Ali beat Frazier in the Garden, Video Techniques had Foreman defending his title against Ken Norton in Caracas, Venezuela. Schwartz and Burnstein had a lot of trouble with that one. Foreman was not an easy man to handle and on the day of the fight he claimed he hurt his leg and was not going to fight. Actually, he was unhappy because, for the first time, he had learned that the Venezuelan government was going to put a sizeable tax on his purse.

Schwartz and Burnstein were in a panic, but the matter was settled. King claimed that he had straightened everything out. He did not play up to Sadler anymore, because by that time Foreman's manager had lost face with the champion, who blamed Sadler for his problems in Caracas.

When they finally got Foreman into the ring with Norton, it was hardly a fight. Foreman flattened Norton in two rounds. That's when the real struggle began. The next day Foreman was stopped at the airport in Caracas by customs because of nonpayment of certain taxes. Some of Video Techniques' equipment was impounded, too. It was a mess. Foreman looked at Sadler with daggers in his eyes.

In New York, I heard about the problem and laughed. One thing about boxing. If something happens it takes about a minute and a half for the news to travel around the world. How it travels, I don't know, but it travels.

About this time I was trying to make a match between Muhammad Ali and Jerry Quarry. It was a hot match because Ali had just beaten Frazier and Quarry had knocked out Don King's hero, Earnie Shavers, in one round. Herbert Muhammad was interested in the match. But when Don King got back from Caracas, he started to booby-trap my fight. First, he went suckıng around Herbert Muhammad. Then he started operating with Video Techniques.

While this was going on, I was pressing Ali and his manager for a deal on the Quarry match. Finally, they agreed to the fight and we invited the press to a conference the next day to announce that Ali would fight Quarry in Madison Square Garden.

I kept hearing that Ali wasn't going to take the fight because Video Techniques had an offer of a $12 million package for a title fight in Kinshasa, Zaire, between Foreman and Ali. I was fuming. Here we had a press conference scheduled the next day and Herbert Muhammad was holding hands with Video Techniques, through King. I couldn't believe that anybody would pay $12 million for a fight, much less the government of Zaire.

I knew that Ali was in town and staying at Herbert Muhammad's apartment on Central Park South, a couple of miles up from the Garden. So I jumped into a cab and rode up there, and went to Herbert's apartment.

As I went into the apartment, Drew Brown, who was called Bundini and worked with Ali, whispered to me, "Don King is in the bedroom. He's hiding there."

I said to Herbert, "What about the Quarry fight? You're supposed to be at a press conference tomorrow to announce it." Ali came into the room and sat on a couch. Herbert said, "What would you say, Teddy, if I told you I can get $5 million for Ali to fight Foreman in Zaire?"

At first I wanted to laugh. Then I said, "Herbert, if you can get $5 million to fight Foreman, grab it, because George Foreman is not going to beat Ali no matter what people think. And $5 million is a lot of money, certainly more than the million you're going to get to fight Jerry Quarry. But if Don King is around and made you that offer, I wish he'd come out from wherever he is and at least announce himself."

136

There was no movement, so I hollered at the top of my lungs, "Don King, if you're in the building, come out!" But he never came out. He stayed in the bedroom and I left. When they signed the match, Schwartz and Burnstein had a lot to do with it. King, it turned out, just worked for them.

"We needed a black interface to make it easier for us with Foreman and Ali." Burnstein said. "We had King with us for that purpose." That was computer talk, but I knew what he meant

Ali knocked out Foreman in eight rounds. He lay on the ropes, doing his rope-a-dope thing, and Foreman punched himself out. Then Ali went to work on Foreman and flattened him. Everybody called it an upset. I didn't. Foreman really never learned how to fight.

By the time Ali made the first defense of the title he had held before, King had entrenched his position with Herbert Muhammad. They were pals, even if Video Techniques was still involved in the promotion of Ali's fights. But Schwartz and Burnstein lasted only two more bouts with Ali. When Ali defended his title against Joe Bugner in Kuala Lumpur in July 1975, King had a lock on the promotion of the champion's bouts.

16

The Top of a Tall Tower

Mike Burke came to the Garden in July 1973, after George Steinbrenner fired him as president of the Yankees. By that time Gulf and Western had gained control of the Garden and Jim Judelson, the president of the conglomerate, liked Burke. I couldn't care less, one way or the other. I was a matchmaker and the only thing I knew about the executive suite was that it was usually at the top of a tall tower. In the Garden, the boxing department was on the first floor.

Right from the start, I learned one thing. Burke knew as much about boxing as he knew about baseball, and everybody knew that while he was running the Yankees, they finished out of money every year. That wasn't my business. But when Burke agreed to meet a committee of managers who were complaining about my matchmaking style, I got mad, really mad.

What the managers told Burke was that they were unhappy because the matches I made were too tough. "They're too even-up," a manager told Burke. "We can't build up our fighters that way."

When I heard this, I told Burke off. I said it wasn't my job to build up fighters. What I wanted in Madison Square Garden were fights that were competitive. "The Garden is the best-known boxing arena in the world," I said. "Fighters should be developed in smaller clubs, not in the Garden. When they get to the Garden, they should be stars."

Burke wasn't my kind of guy. Funny thing about him, he had class. He was a great guy at a party or in public relations. I never knew a sportswriter who knocked him. But when it came right down to making a match, he knew nothing about how to work with managers or how to figure percentages.

When the Garden had Ali and Norton in their third fight, in Yankee Stadium in 1976, Burke decided that he would shut me out of the negotiations for the match. He was very friendly at the time with Bob Arum and Arum was in as the Garden's partner because he could deliver Ali.

After the match was closed, I learned that Ali had been guaranteed $6 million. I couldn't argue with that, because Ali was the world heavyweight champion and without him there would be no show. But then I heard that Norton was guaranteed a purse of $1 million, plus 5 percent of the net gate and television receipts. I blew my top.

I wrote a note to Burke telling him how I felt. I said that while $6 million was still a lot of money, even for Ali, he would earn every penny of it by going out and getting a lot of stuff on the sports pages. Then I asked Burke how he could justify Norton's terms, which wound up with Norton getting $1.5 million finally. I said, in so many words, that Norton's manager, Bob Biron, would have accepted the fight for half a million. "You're overpaying him," I told Burke.

The fight grossed $8.5 million, counting the gate and the proceeds from closed-circuit TV and foreign markets. But the

Garden and Arum lost $600,000, only because Burke let himself be talked into paying Norton a million dollars more than he was worth.

A year later another thing happened that cost the Garden a bundle. This time it was Ali's fight with Earnie Shavers that put everybody in the middle, including me. The way I remember it, the whole thing could have been prevented if Burke had acted fast in a ticklish situation.

In May 1977, we signed Ali to a contract to fight Duane Bobick. The fight was to be part of a double-header in which Norton would fight Ron Lyle on the same card. But after the contract was signed, Ali announced one of his numerous retirements. The reason for that "retirement" was Ali's reluctance to fight Bobick, who was white. People kept telling him, "Man you gonna fight a tough dude and he gonna whip your black ass, and he's white." At least that's what I heard.

So Ali pulled out of the match with Bobick and there was nothing we could do about it because of his retirement announcement. Instead of the double-header, we shifted plans. We put Bobick in with Ken Norton, and at last the terms were reasonable.

I got Norton for a flat fee of $500,000, twice as much as Bobick signed for. Then the Garden sold the rights to the fight to NBC-TV for $1.5 million. We did not black out New York, yet the match drew $300,000 at the box office. This brought the total receipts to $1.8 million. The Garden's profit came to more than $800,000. It was a big score. Norton knocked out Bobick in the first round, bombing him with punches to the head. Almost immediately, Ali announced that his retirement was over.

With the news, I went after Ali and got him to accept Earnie Shavers as a challenger in exchange for $2.5 million. I called Frank Luca in Ohio and asked him if he would let Shavers fight Ali for the title. "I can get you $200,000," I said. "Sounds

141

all right with me," Luca said. He was Shavers's trainer, but at the time he was doing the fighter's business too.

"Frank, send me a telegram saying you accept the match," I told him.

"Teddy, that's okay, but we'll need to get $30,000 up front," Luca said.

"I think I can get the people in the building to go for $20,000," I said. "I don't know about the $30,000. Anyway, send me a telegram accepting the match."

I let Burke know about the deal and about the $30,000 advance to Shavers. "I'll think about it," he said. Meanwhile, we sent Luca a check for $10,000 just to hold him. When the telegram came, I thought everything was all right with the match. I still hadn't heard from Burke about the rest of the $30,000 advance and couldn't get any authority to send $20,000 more to Luca.

Burke was a funny guy that way. He didn't seem to be able to make a quick decision. You could go up to his office and talk to him and swap jokes, and maybe that was the trouble. Getting him to say yes or no was a tough thing.

While I was waiting on Burke, Bob Arum heard about our plan for an Ali-Shavers bout. He was as mad as hell. He had shared the losses with the Garden on the Ali-Norton bout and felt that the least the Garden could do was to give him a piece of Ali's bout with Shavers.

Arum called Luca and asked him if he had signed a contract for the Ali fight. "No, but I sent Teddy a telegram. I asked them to advance us $30,000. Teddy offered me $20,000 and sent me $10,000. I'm still waiting."

"We'll get together," Arum told Luca, and when they met, Arum offered Luca $300,000 for a bout with Ali. What is more, he said he would advance Shavers $30,000 immediately. Luca signed with Arum.

Now the Garden was in a hell of a fix. We had the con-

142

tract with Ali but we weren't sure of Shavers. We asked the New York State Athletic Commission to rule on the matter, and Floyd Patterson, a member of the commission, conducted a hearing at which Luca admitted sending a telegram to me accepting the Ali bout. Patterson ruled that the telegram was acceptable as a contract in the circumstances.

Arum did not give up easily. He went into a state court in New York to stop us from using Shavers, claiming he had a contract for the fighter's services. We sought relief in a federal court. People started to call each other names and a lot of bad mouthing went on. The State Supreme Court decided that the Garden had no contract with Shavers. We won in the federal court.

It was a draw and we were on the spot. The contract with Ali was only an option agreement. If we could not deliver a contract on Shavers within a few months, Ali would be free to fight for another promoter. Burke panicked. He guaranteed Ali the $2.5 million even if the fight did not take place. And we signed Shavers, only he got $300,000 instead of the original $200,000. But the matter was still in the courts and Arum was sure of his grounds.

We were up a creek when the U.S. Court of Appeals reversed our win in the federal district court. The case was now back in the state court, where Arum had won before. Burke met with Arum's lawyer, Theodore H. Friedman. They argued and Friedman walked out.

There was concern in the executive suite on the 18th floor at 2 Penn Plaza, where the Garden brass worked. Alan N. Cohen was running the store for Gulf and Western, and he was worried about the way things were going. Our lawyers met with Arum's lawyers and a deal was made. Case dismissed. Arum's company, Top Rank, was guaranteed $300,000. The Garden, which paid a couple of hundred thousand in legal fees, went for the extra $100,000 for Shavers's purse.

We did all right, because NBC-TV paid $4 million for the

live telecast. And it turned out to be a hell of a fight. Shavers kept pressing Ali through the entire fifteen rounds and could have got it, if the officials weren't in love with Ali's fancy moves. The next day, at a press conference in the Garden, I told Ali to hang up his gloves. The *New York Post* had a front-page headline big as your right arm. It said: "GARDEN BOSS TO ALI: QUIT!"

Ali didn't take my advice, of course, but I felt I could speak my mind. I never gave him a song and a dance, like most of the people around him. I like to think I started him as a pro and I never let him get into a position to look bad.

Whenever Ali fought for the Garden, he fought tough opponents. I didn't put him in with Chuck Wepner or Jean-Pierre Coopman or Richard Dunn, or in with a wrestler named Antonio Inoki in Tokyo. The matches I made for him were competitive. He had no picnic with Joe Frazier in their two Garden fights, or with Ken Norton at Yankee Stadium, or with Earnie Shavers, who must have hit him a hundred good shots. And he had to fight to beat Oscar Bonavena in the Garden.

A fight doesn't have to be a tank job to be a fraud. If one fighter has a great advantage over another fighter going in, that to me is not a fight, it's a walkover. Like I said before, I made only one of them in my life.

I have a good friend named Abe Margolies, who is a jeweler in New York. He is a very rich man who loves sports and once I convinced him to manage a young Puerto Rican boxer named Pedro Soto. Soto was one of those early bloomers. He started out as a middleweight in the amateurs and pretty soon was a light-heavyweight, which he was when Abe Margolies took him over. But as he got heavy, he lost his skills. I found that out the hard way.

There are no secrets in boxing and when Margolies became Soto's manager, everybody in the business winked, like they knew something. And every time I made a match for Soto, they came to see whether I was giving him a soft touch because his manager was my friend. Some people in boxing even said I had a piece of the action. I have to say again that I never had a piece of any fighter, not Soto or anybody else.

Soto looked great in his first pro fights, and then I put him in with Jerry Quarry's brother, Mike, and he lost a close decision. One night he was on the card in the Garden and the fellow he was supposed to fight pulled out. So I called in an old warhorse named Bill Douglas from Ohio. The knockers said I was getting Soto an old broken-down opponent. Douglas gave Soto a terrible beating. So I became the laughing stock of boxing, but it didn't bother me because they could not say I was giving Soto soft touches.

I had a hell of a time with Soto. Here was Margolies, my friend, managing him and here I was getting him knocked off, and all the time boxing people were saying I was trying to protect him. Sure I wanted to protect him, but only from getting hurt. When he showed that he was making no progress in boxing and stood to get hurt, I advised Margolies to retire him. He did. But when I advised Ali to quit, he didn't take my advice. There was too much money in it for him, and the proof of that was in his last fight, when he got $8 million for fighting Larry Holmes in Las Vegas and quit in his corner. He was through, but there were people around him willing to use him.

People are always being used in boxing. People have tried to use me, but I resisted them. I can't use names here, but I want to tell you about a very good fighter from Italy who was managed by a couple of his relatives. One day the managers came to me in the Garden and when they entered my office, they closed the door behind them. Niether of the two spoke English, so they brought an interpreter with them.

Through the interpreter, they said they would like to get a bout for their fighter in Madison Square Garden. I knew the fighter. He was no bum, and I said, "Hey, sure, we'd like to use him." The managers said, "We'd like to fight two fights, and then maybe fight Emile Griffith for the championship." They said, "The two fights—the first fight you must be very careful, you must make sure we win in three rounds, no more. The other fellow must fall down in three rounds. The second fight in three or four rounds. Then we fight for the championship."

I said, "Listen, you fucking bums, open that door. It opens the same way it did when you came in. Get the hell out of here and don't ever come back. As far as I'm concerned your fighter will never fight in Madison Square Garden. Now fuck off."

The shame of it was that the fighter was colorful and would have been a great attraction in the Garden, if he fought on the level.

That wasn't the only time I got a proposition from a European manager. Another time I went to San Remo, Italy, for a fight between Don Fullmer and Nino Benvenuti for the middleweight title. While I was on the Italian Riviera, this European manager came to me and said, "You know I'm more than a manager, I'm a promoter, and I'd like to have my middleweight to fight Dick Tiger for the title. Can you arrange it, Mr. Brenner?"

"I can, if the fight takes place in Madison Square Garden," I said. "We'll talk about terms and work everything out."

"No, I don't want the fight to take place in Madison Square Garden," the European manager said. "I want Dick Tiger to come to my country to fight."

"In that case," I said, "I'll give you the name of Dick Tiger's manager, I'll give you his phone number, and you can get in touch with him, and if he wants to come into your country, if the conditions are right, I guess you can make a match."

"Oh, but I wish you would talk to the manager," he said.

"What do you want me to talk to him about?"

He said, "Well, I want Dick Tiger to fall down in the fourth round. I want to make sure. He has to lose. Because if he doesn't lose, it is no good for my fighter and for me."

I looked this bum in the eye and said, "If you ever put

that proposition up to Dick Tiger or his manager, they'll hit you right on top of your head. Don't try it."

I wouldn't fix a fight for my own brother. That doesn't mean that everybody in boxing feels that way. But I've met some great guys in boxing and made some good friends. And many of them had more on the ball and more goodness in their hearts than people in high places.

Putting that down, I think of Leroy Nieman and a story he once told me. Nieman is an artist with a wonderful flair for colors and a great feeling for sports. Years ago he was commissioned by Irving Mitchell Felt to paint a fight scene at the Garden.

What Nieman did was to paint a montage of hundreds of faces around ringside, including one hundred and twenty-six recognizable faces of promoters, managers, boxing reporters, and prominent New Yorkers.

When the canvas, measuring nine by twelve feet, was completed, Nieman invited Felt to his studio to see it. "It's great," Felt said, "but I'd like a couple of changes."

"Like what?" Nieman asked.

"Well, I'd like you to take out the faces of Frank Costello and Frankie Carbo."

"I know they're mobsters," Nieman said, "but they're part of the fight scene. Costello used to come to the Garden regularly on fight nights, and Carbo controlled more fighters than anybody else."

"But they're gangsters and I don't want them in the painting," Felt said.

"As you say," Nieman said, and using several strokes of a brush to alter the faces of Costello and Carbo, he converted them into two famous New York politicians. He said, "Somehow that seemed to work better than any other way."

That painting cost the Garden $18,000. It is now worth at least $100,000. It hangs in Room 200 at the Garden, where the corporation's brass entertain their friends and associates before sporting events in the arena. Nobody there knows that Costello and Carbo look down upon the social scene disguised as politicians. That's Madison Square Garden for you.

And So It Ends

When Harry Markson retired as president of Madison Square Garden Boxing, Inc., in March 1973, I was handed the title. It was a dirty trick. I didn't want the job and I didn't need it, but when I heard from Muhammad Ali I felt pretty good about it. Ali wasn't the champion then. He was at his camp in Deer Lake, Pa., training for his second fight with Ken Norton when I got a telegram from him. It said, "Dear Teddy, I wish to congratulate you on your new position. You are truly a credit to boxing. I'm looking forward to making your job successful when I participate in boxing for you and Madison Square Garden. It takes a great man to recognize a great man."

That pleased me, but it didn't take the curse off my new job. I could never be a boss, not even in boxing, because of the way I grew up in the game. When I came into boxing all a man needed was the telephone number at Stillman's Gym. He kept his business under his hat and got his calls at the gym.

In the gym, I remember, there were two guys named Kelly. That wasn't their right names. They just took it because it sounded good. So one day the phone rang in a booth at Stillman's Gym and the fellow who answered asked the caller, "Which Kelly do you want, the Italian Kelly or the Jewish Kelly?"

The additional job in the Garden kept me pinned to my desk and I didn't like the paperwork. I didn't like making decisions about how much a secretary should get paid and things like that. I wanted to sit around and swap lies with the boys, and if I had to run around all night to make a fight, I'd do it. But those other things bothered me.

Markson was still connected with the Garden. When he retired, Irving Mitchell Felt arranged for him to be retained as a consultant to the boxing department. But that was a part-time thing and the day-to-day decisions he used to make now fell on my shoulders. I can't tell you how much I missed him.

I used to kid him a lot about the way he loved good music, but when I got a record or a tape by a great artist I would make sure it got to Markson. He was a cultured guy in a tough racket, and he had guts. Nobody could put the bull on him. When Jim Norris was running the Garden and Markson was the director of boxing, Markson really showed he had guts.

What happened was that when Markson arrived at his office in the old Garden one morning, he was greeted by the matchmaker, a fellow named Billy Brown, who was very close to Carbo. Brown told Markson, "I got to make a return between Gavilan and Jones."

"You what?"

"The boss wants me to make a return between Gavilan and Jones."

"Listen, let me tell you something, Billy," Markson said. "I saw Kid Gavilan and Tiger Jones in that fight in Florida and it was a terrible fight. I don't want them fighting again."

"I got orders from the boss," the matchmaker said.

150

"Billy, I don't want you to make that fight until I have a chance to talk to Mr. Norris. It just stinks. I don't want it here."

Markson knew of Gavilan's connections. In fact, everybody in boxing knew that Frankie Carbo had a piece of Gavilan, who had lost the decision to Jones in their fight in Miami. What they wanted was a return bout for Gavilan to get a win over Jones to wipe out the loss in Miami.

A while later, Norris called in from his home in Coral Gables, Florida. Markson got on the phone and said, "Jim, Billy Brown tells me you want to make a return match between Kid Gavilan and Tiger Jones and I told him not to dare make the fight until I had a chance to talk to you. Jim, it just stinks, and I don't want the fight in the Garden."

What Markson did not realize was that the phones in the Garden's boxing department were being tapped by the district attorney. A while later, during a grand jury investigation of boxing, Markson received a subpoena to testify. When he appeared before the grand jury, the first thing an assistant D.A. named Alfred Scotti asked him concerned the Gavilan-Jones fight.

"It did stink," Markson said. "I didn't want the fight and I told Mr. Norris I didn't want the fight."

The mob got its way, anyway. Two months after Jones beat Gavilan in Miami, they fought again in Philadelphia. This time Gavilan won the decision. Markson smelled a rat. Anyone in boxing as long as he gets very sensitive about bad smells.

It takes a boxing guy to handle a boxing situation. A guy might be a great success in one field and get mugged in boxing. When Sonny Werblin took over in January 1978, as president of Madison Square Garden Corporation, I thought about that. Werblin was not a stranger to me. He was my *landsman*. He had played sports at James Madison, the Brooklyn high school I went to. He was big in show business and had owned pieces of Monmouth Park race track in New Jersey and the New York Jets. A believer in the "star" system, he had signed Joe Namath for $427,000 to play for the Jets.

He was a hard-working guy who wouldn't let go once he got started on something. The way he put over the Meadowlands Sports Complex in New Jersey proved that. For a long time people said the project, which included the construction of a racetrack and a football stadium for the New York Giants, seemed doomed by financial problems. But Werblin kept at it and got the financing straightened out. When he left the state-operated complex late in 1977 for Madison Square Garden, it was a very successful sports enterprise paying more than its own way.

At first I looked forward to working with Werblin, but then I began to wonder. He was in the Garden for three weeks, maybe a whole month, before I even got to see him. Even then, I had to make the first move. We had a fight coming up between Wilfred Benitez, who was the junior welterweight champion, and Bruce Curry, a pretty good kid out of California. I phoned Werblin's office and asked him to attend a luncheon for the press, where he could have his picture taken with the fighters.

He came down to the Hall of Fame room in the Garden and we shook hands. "We ought to sit down and talk," he said. That was all.

Pretty soon I heard stories that bothered me. Don King was going around town telling people he was going to take over the Garden from me. At first I didn't believe it, but then things began happening. I went to see Werblin and told him that Wilfred Benitez's contract was for sale; did he know of anybody who would be interested in managing the world junior welterweight champion? Werblin said he knew nobody who would be interested. /

So I went to my friend Abe Margolies and asked him if he wanted to handle Benitez. "It'll cost you about $75,000," I told Abe. He said it sounded interesting, but why he would be interested I couldn't figure out. He had managed two fighters before. Pedro Soto had been a great disappointment to him. Before that, he had bought a Texas heavyweight named Jim Elder, who developed a tumor of the brain and died without once fighting for Abe.

Now there was Benitez up for sale because his father, Gregorio Benitez, needed the money. Gregorio Benitez was in horses. He played them and owned them, and when things went bad, he decided to sell the contract on his son. Part of the reason was that he found it tough to train his son, who wasn't yet twenty years old at the time but very interested in pleasure. He thought if another manager had Wilfred, the kid would listen to him more than to a father.

So that's how come I asked Margolies to buy the fighter. Then I wrote Gregorio Benitez a letter in which I outlined the deal. First, Margolies would lend Gregorio $5,000, which would be applied to the purchase of the fighter's contract. There would be another payment of $10,000, followed by still another of $45,000. The total would be $60,000. In addition, Margolies would wipe out a $16,000 debt made up of money advanced to the fighter by the Garden.

"Mr. Margolies and Wilfred," I wrote, "will have a standard New York contract in which the expenses come off the top, then Wilfred receives 66 2/3 per cent and Mr. Margolies receives 33 1/3 per cent" of all purses.

The deal fell through because, after thinking it over, I said to Margolies, "Walk away, Abe. It's not for you. After all, the father will always be around and if you want to make a match he doesn't want, he'll tell his son don't take it, and you've got trouble."

So Margolies took a walk and I spoke to Jimmy Jacobs about it. Jacobs loves boxing. He has the finest collection of fight films in the world and his company produces things like *The*

Greatest Fights of the Century and other television features. I knew Jacobs had the money and could swing the deal for Benitez. He did. And what a deal he made. His profit on a $75,000 investment has brought him maybe three quarters of a million, with more to come. It was a hell of a deal, but it didn't work out so good for me. After I asked Werblin if he knew anybody who wanted to buy Benitez's contract, I heard that he was knocking my brains out for getting involved in the whole thing to begin with. What he seemed to mean was that I was in cahoots with Margolies to grab the fighter for myself. I got real mad, but not as mad as I was when the Garden finally announced that King would be the co-promoter of a series of fights in the Garden.

"Tell Teddy," Werblin told Harry Markson, "not to be worried. The King thing doesn't affect him. He can be in the Garden as long as he wants the job."

"Sit tight," Markson told me. "After all, you're still the president of Madison Square Garden Boxing."

I tried to keep cool, because I knew that King had sold Werblin a bill of goods. What King had worked on was the idea that he had Larry Holmes, the WBC heavyweight champion, under an exclusive service contract, along with many other fighters. The Garden could not sign fighters to exclusive services because the old antitrust decree was still in effect.

What King did not tell Werblin was that fighters simply refused to fight in New York because of heavy state taxes. That was an old story, going back to 1974, when I was trying to make a fight for Joe Frazier in the Garden. At that time I got a letter from Bruce Wright, Frazier's attorney, in which he said that the problem of fighting in New York was taxes. Frazier had just knocked out Jerry Quarry in five rounds in the Garden and Wright pointed out that the taxes paid to the state by the fighter, his trainer, and the fighter's corporation, Cloverlay, had come to $37,007.82, or 9 percent of the gross for the fight. "The tax is just uneconomic," the lawyer wrote me. "We are anxious to fight

154

in New York," Wright said. "It is the best place to have fights. It is also the worst place to pay taxes."

Werblin was not aware of the tax situation when he hooked up with King. What he did was to make the announcement of their association at an all-day outing at a golf club in Eastchester, Westchester County. The bill for the party came to $13,000 which the Garden paid. At first I didn't want to attend, but Werblin insisted that I sit at the same table with King. I did, but we didn't talk. Neither did Werblin ask me to make a speech. When newspapermen asked me about the new arrangement, I let them know that I was not happy with it. It got into the papers and this did not sit well with Werblin.

Actually, I wouldn't have minded working with King, except that he made it impossible. He went around giving stories out to newspapermen throughout the world that he was the sole boss of boxing in the Garden. It wasn't true, because there is one thing you have to understand. I was still the Garden's matchmaker and as long as I was, I had to approve the quality of the fights he was putting into the building.

That wasn't the worst part of it. Even while King was putting shows into the Garden, I was making matches for my own shows in the place. I found myself competing with King for the same fighters. I'd call up a manager and offer him fifteen or twenty thousand for his fighter's services and he'd say, "King just offered me the same fight for much more money."

I got to Werblin and I told him, "How can we possibly do business under such an arrangement!" Finally, I tried to make a match between Alfredo Escalera, the former World Boxing Council junior lightweight champion, and Julio (Diabilito) Valdez, a good Dominican fighter. King complained to Werblin that he had an exclusive on Escalera's services.

When I told Werblin that Paul Ruiz, Escalera's manager, would verify that the fighter had no ties to King, Sonny suggested that I arrange for him to meet the manager.

"Tell you what," I told Werblin. "Escalera and his manager are coming to our next show in the Garden. Why can't you see them that night?"

He agreed, but on the night of the fight, I noticed that Werblin and Burke were not in the arena. About ten o'clock I got word that they were having dinner at Mike Manuche's on West 52nd Street and were expecting me to bring Escalera and his manager to the restaurant after the show. We had a little trouble in the Garden that night—a sort of minor riot over a disputed decision—and when I got to Mike Manuche's I told Werblin I was sorry it happened. "No problem," he said. "Forget it."

We all sat around a large table—Werblin, Burke, myself, Escalera, and Paul Ruiz and a girlfriend he brought with him. It didn't take long for Ruiz to verify that Escalera had no ties to King and was a free agent. Everybody listened, and then I noticed Werblin calling the headwaiter and speaking to him. In a second, from the other side of the restaurant, I saw King and his lawyer, Bob Tofel, approaching our table. Now I knew I was in a trap. They sat down and because I was almost at the head of the table, where we had eight people seated, I had a hard time moving. Finally I decided that by stepping up on my chair and then almost walking across the table, I could get out.

"I don't have to sit here and listen to this bullshit," I said over my shoulder. Werblin's and Burke's eyes popped as I walked out of the joint. I expected to hear from Werblin the next day, which was the Friday before Labor Day, but I heard from Burke instead. He called and said he wanted to see me. "I'm coming down to your office," he said. "I'll go up to yours," I suggested. He came down to my office.

"I don't know how to tell you this," Burke said.

"Just tell it to me," I said. "What's on your mind?"

"Sonny would like to terminate you in Madison Square Garden," he said.

"Well, go right ahead," I said. "I've been here a long time. Twenty years. I'm not going to cry about it." And that's the way it ended.

A Homer Is Better Than a Triple

The Labor Day weekend was tough, but Judy and I tried to forget that for the first time in twenty years I was out of work. We had moved into Manhattan from Brooklyn a few years before and our co-op apartment, off Fifth Avenue, was right in the middle of town. On holidays, the streets are mostly clear and it is pleasant to walk up and down the avenue looking in store windows and just feeling good.

That is exactly what my wife and I did that weekend, but on Tuesday, when I left my apartment to go down to the Garden, it dawned on me that I would be there for the last time. I had a lot of things to clear out of my desk, and there was a huge oil painting of Benny Leonard on a wall that I had to get back to the great lightweight champion's brother, who had lent it to me.

As soon as I walked into the Garden, I met an old friend. "Geez, it's too bad," Gil Clancy said. "I know you're out. I've been offered your job as matchmaker. Should I take it?"

"Should you take it, you horse's ass? Of course, you should take it. If you don't they'll give it to somebody else."

I couldn't help thinking, here's a guy for whom I took

157

some bum raps because I used Emile Griffith in so many fights, and now he takes over my job as matchmaker in the Garden. I didn't stay in the building very long. I got my things and left.

Now I had to think about what I was going to do. Naturally, I wasn't going to leave boxing. It was my game and I loved it, and what the hell else was I going to do? I went to see Alan Lubell. He owned a television production company called Marathon Entertainment, Inc., and some years before, when he had been Eddie Einhorn's associate at TVS, I made a deal with TVS to get a series of seven fight shows on an independent television network. When Einhorn, who now owns a big piece of the Chicago White Sox, sold TVS for several million dollars, Lubell organized his own company, which he called Marathon Entertainment.

I made a deal with Lubell to promote fights for television, and I got in touch with Dr. Eduardo Roman, a Nicaraguan lawyer who was the manager of Alexis Arguello, the WBC junior lightweight champion. We had been friends for a long time. Arguello had fought for me in the Garden three or four times before becoming the junior lightweight champion, and I had gone on record as saying he was the best fighter in the world, pound for pound. A month after I left the Garden, Arguello and Dr. Roman gave me the exclusive promotional rights to Arguello's fights for two years. I had to go to Nicaragua in the middle of a revolution to get it, but I was in business.

The first championship bout I made for Arguello matched him against the former champion Escalera. They had fought before and Arguello had won the championship by knocking Escalera out in the thirteenth round. I went to CBS and sold the title fight to the network for $240,000. And I scheduled it for Rimini, Italy.

The next thing I knew, Don King was in the act, claiming that he had the right to promote the màtch between Arguello and Escalera. When he put CBS on notice, the network notified me that it was cancelling the contract for the Arguello-Escalera bout. I went to ABC-TV and tried to sell the fight there instead. I could have predicted what would happen next because José Sulaiman had stated that the World Boxing Council would not sanction the Arguello-Escalera bout unless I reached an "understanding" with King.

I was over a barrel, because I knew ABC-TV would not televise the fight if it wasn't sanctioned by the WBC. I had to do something fast, and I knew that the only way to avoid more complications was to make a deal with King. I agreed to pay him $25,000 for a compromise of the situation. This meant that in exchange for the $25,000, King would give up any claims he had to the Arguello-Escalera match. Lubell sent him a check for the full amount.

On the eve of the fight, I got word that something funny was going on. King claimed, in a letter to the WBC, that he had the rights to Arguello's next two fights, if Arguello remained champion. What a crock that was. Alan Lubell stopped payment on the $25,000 check we had given to King. And we notified King and Sulaiman that we knew horseshit when we saw it.

The fight between Arguello and Escalera went thirteen rounds. It was such a good fight, the WBC named it the "WBC Fight of the Year" for 1979. Three months after the bout, Sulaiman notified me that I had "been suspended as a boxing promoter for WBC world title fights" because I had gone through with the promotion of the Arguello bout without reaching an agreement with King.

The suspension came out of the blue. I hired a lawyer and I filed a suit in the United States District Court, for the Southern District of New York to get the WBC off my back.

When I filed my suit against the World Boxing Council, the first thing my lawyer did was to ask for a preliminary injunction that would reinstate me as a promoter. The WBC hired Edward Bennett Williams's law firm to represent it, which made me feel good. It proved I had the WBC worried. Once in court, Judge William C. Conner indicated that there was no basis for the suspension and the WBC agreed to reinstate me. By that time, however, Arguello's contract with me wasn't worth very much, because I had failed to promote three title bouts for him in the first year of our contract. Instead of promoting on my own, I went to work in Bob Arum's office. The circle had been closed.

There was Clancy sitting in my old chair in the Garden and here I was working for Arum. King's association with Werblin and the Garden did not last very long. He co-promoted only five shows in Madison Square Garden. I'll bet Werblin was glad to be rid of him when their agreement expired.

When I got into boxing, a promoter was a man who put his own money on the line and went out and sold tickets to a fight. If it was not an attractive match, the promoter blew a bundle. But at least he operated on his own. Now a promoter can make a fight and go out and sell it to TV, and is almost assured of a profit before he sells a single ticket. Television proceeds make the difference.

Nothing that happens in boxing surprises me. In my years in the business, I have seen investigations by the federal government, Congress, district attorneys. People have gone to the can for things they have done in boxing. But Sulaiman takes the cake. He tried to knock me out of the box and succeeded only in keeping a lot of lawyers busy and costing me a lot of money. But what the WBC is doing to boxing itself is worse.

I'm not an old guy thinking the old days were better. It isn't easy staying young enough to remember what things in boxing were like when you were really young. In those days we had good fighters and bad fighters, like we have them now, but I like to think the good ones got their shots when they deserved the chance. Now, the way the game is being run, a kid doesn't have a chance unless he makes the right connection.

It's like choosing the right doctor when you're sick. Not long ago I discovered that I had a problem with my heart. I thought that was a funny thing because being in boxing makes you judge all guys by their physical conditions, especially fighters. Now here I was with a heart problem. I went to the hospital and had a quadruple bypass. That's where they take blood vessels from your legs and transplant them. Funny thing, I feel better than ever.

When I was in the hospital, I got a call from Robby Margolies, who is Abe Margolies's brother. Robby said, "What the hell are you doing?" I said, "What the hell am I doing! I just had a quadruple bypass, but that's not bad, because a home run is better than a triple."

"I didn't ask you how you feel," Robby Margolies said. "I asked you what you were doing?"

"What am I doing?" I screamed. "Listen, I never had it so good. I have two pro football games on two television sets right in front of me and I bet a couple of dollars on each game. Gives me a chance to root for something. What more can a guy ask for?"

I have other things to root for. I root for my son, Dr. Richard P. Brenner, who is a neurologist at the medical center of the University of New Mexico in Albuquerque, and my daughter, Mrs. Marsha A. Gardner, who trained at the Sorbonne in Paris and teaches French at a prep school in Berkeley, California. What makes me mention them and the four wonderful grandchildren they have given Judy and me is to prove that people in boxing are real and have families and do not spend their lives in sewers. Being in it is not exactly like being a rabbi, but, like they used to say, it beats stealing. I had a lot of laughs and answered a lot of questions. The answers I didn't give, I didn't know. They will never be found between the covers of a book, not even this one.

Index

163

164

DISCARDED